REIGN FALLS DOWN

STEVEN B. HARRIS

EDITED BY AMY J. NELSON

BOOK COVER DESIGN BY CLAUDIA SEBATIANY

claudiasebastiany.com

REIGN
FALLS
DOWN

DEDICATION

I want to extend a "thank you" to my two most valued relationships.

God and my beautiful wife, Jill. You have helped me fulfill a bucket list through endless love, inspiration, patience, and grace when I didn't deserve it. You both give my life purpose. This book was not possible without your strength. I love and need you both in my life.

PROLOGUE

"One man pretends to be rich, yet has nothing;
another pretends to be poor, yet has great wealth."

TWO YEARS EARLIER HARRISON AND CLAIRE MARKS WERE LIVING IN their two-bedroom apartment. The newlyweds settled in Broad Ripple, Indiana. The town offered great restaurants and nightlife that appealed to most young couples, but not for these two career-focused professionals.

They often congregated in the bedroom as night began to fall. Harrison turned on the television only to drown out the noise coming from the apartment next door. The couple shared their day and scrolled through mobile devices while stretched on the king size bed too big for the tiny bedroom.

"Check this out, Claire," Harrison exclaimed half irritated. "My dad is finally returning my call."

Both rolled their eyes and wondered whose birthday was approaching they may have overlooked. They didn't see any events on their social calendar.

Harrison hadn't seen his father in nearly two months. Typically, if it weren't a special occasion, the family wouldn't get together or even text or talk on the phone. It was foolish to expect random invitations to his father's house as the elder Marks centered on their social agenda. The last time the young couple dropped in for a surprise visit, they were asked to call first.

Harrison didn't mind the emotional distance. Visits with his father were often uncomfortable since the two didn't have much in common. Therefore, it was with great surprise when Harrison saw the call come through. He left his dad a message five weeks earlier to share the news of his job promotion, but his father never returned the call.

Harlan Marks didn't bother much with greetings. Once Harrison answered, Harlan launched into his conversation.

"Victoria and I want to meet with you as soon as possible," his father said enthusiastically.

"What did we do wrong?" his son said hoping to get a rise out of his father.

Passive aggressive. Not a good trait, Harrison thought to himself.

Regardless, he knew this had nothing to do with his stepmother's desire to meet. Victoria, his father's wife of three years, didn't want anything to do with Harrison unless it included writing him out of the will.

Harlan didn't miss a beat. "Ha! Nothing yet. When do you think the two of you can come?"

Harrison knew the old man would want to play host. There wasn't a chance his father and his unfriendly wife were going to stop by their apartment. Victoria wouldn't dare step foot into a multi-family complex for a social visit.

Harrison pretended to check his calendar. He knew they had nothing going on for the next month. Going out with friends proved too costly for a young couple focused on saving money to purchase a home.

"We can meet you tomorrow night if that works?" Harrison was talking to his dad but looked at Claire for approval.

Claire cringed, but nodded reluctantly. Going over to her in-law's house required mental preparation and 24 hours didn't provide the mandatory time. It would have to work.

"Plan on coming for dinner. Then we'll talk," Harlan added. "See you at six."

Harrison was about to offer his salutations, but his dad already hung up. It was one more chapter in the madness.

Harrison and Claire were gifted at evaluating the behaviors of other people. They both had a communication degree from Butler University to validate the claim. It helped them be more understanding with one another, but not even a behavioral science degree from an Ivy League school could help Harrison deal with his father.

Harrison and Claire arrived the following evening. Although they had been to the house before, each time they were amazed at the 90-acre lake that took center stage in the Hidden Shores community situated in the northwest corner of Indianapolis. All thirty-single-family homes showcased lakefront property with a view of the sparkling water.

When everyone sat down for dinner, Harlan carried the majority of the conversation as small talk was never Victoria's gift. Neither was cooking.

Harrison and Claire kept entertained by staring out the back windows. The outside view was stunning while adding a much needed break from Harlan's latest topic.

The 2,000 square foot, three-bedroom, single-story home featured floor-to-ceiling windows across the back that showcased a view from every room in the open concept dwelling.

Harlan interrupted the silence, "Yep, Victoria and I need to go to Louisville this weekend."

Harlan stared at his 24-year-old son hoping he would bite on the topic.

Harrison ignored the cue. In an immature fashion he enjoyed frustrating his father, and especially Victoria who by this time was glaring across the table. Harrison couldn't compete with the money his father and step-mother flashed, but when it came to getting under people's skin, he could easily hold his own. Claire realized her husband's child-like behavior and bailed Harlan out of the awkward silence.

"What's in Louisville?" she asked much to Harlan's delight.

"Oh, we need to pick up our new Jag," Harlan said trying now to down-play the trip.

"You bought a Jaguar? As in…a car?" Harrison questioned with disgust.

He couldn't disguise his abhorrence earning him another kick in the leg from Claire – his second kick since they arrived.

This is why we're here. The son-of-a-bitch needs a ride to Louisville, Harrison thought to himself. *He offered me dinner so I wouldn't turn him down when he drops the question.*

Surprisingly, the question never came. Harlan completely changed the subject much to Harrison's relief.

After another long pause, Harlan caught his son and daughter-in-law staring at the lake again.

"You like the view?" he inquired.

"It's beautiful," Claire answered.

"How would you like to live here?" asked Victoria. She hadn't said much throughout the evening, but she was all too eager to set the bait.

"Oh, I would just love it," Claire dreamed out loud.

"Well that's why we brought you here. We have an offer you can't refuse," Harlan said applying a horrible Godfather impression.

"What are you talking about?" Harrison inquired.

"Victoria and I are moving to Geist Reservoir," Harlan waited for the younger Marks to be impressed, but they were too pre-occupied with the current proposition.

Harlan wasted no time, "We want to sell this house to you. We have a plan to make it affordable and we want to share it with you. Our proposal includes the pontoon boat. $450,000 is the offer, but here's how it works," Harlan continued. "We'll call it an open ended mortgage."

Claire was in shock. Once Harlan offered the house, she didn't hear anything else he had to say.

Harrison's head was spinning, but he somehow managed to mumble, "What's an open-ended mortgage?"

Harrison and Claire didn't have any experience with home buying, especially homes they couldn't afford. They lived in apartments since the start of college and paying rent was all they knew. A month ago, they toured a home in Carmel, but the young couple didn't take it very seriously.

Harlan went on trying to get the younger Mark's to snap out of their trance. "Victoria and I will act as the bank for this transaction. We know you can't afford a $425,000 home using a traditional bank loan, so we devised an alternative. If you can apply a $15,000 down payment toward this property, our attorney will construct two promissory notes. The first will be for $200,000 over 30 years."

"Time out," Harrison interrupted as he tried to regain feeling in his body. "What's a promissory note?"

"It's simply a contract that says you agree to pay your lender. In this case your lender is me." Harlan was doing all the talking on behalf of Victoria who returned to glaring across the table.

Although she tried to be kind, she went along with her husband who called the shots. Victoria hated the fact she and Harlan could sell the house for more than 30 percent of what she paid and use the profit to purchase a women's Rolex, the new Jaguar, and more.

Harlan stayed the course. "The second note will be for $225,000."

He noticed their confusion and tried to hide his frustration with the younger couple. Had he been negotiating with someone other than his own family he would have stood up and walked out of the room. Harlan needed to simplify the proposal.

"You're going to pay a mortgage payment to Victoria and me based on the first note at $200,000 after you put $15,000 toward a down payment. This helps keep your monthly payment below what you would expect to pay for a home on the open market if you worked the loan through a bank. I, or we," Harlan corrected himself after getting a glare from Victoria, "will delay the responsibility of the second note with zero interest charged to you. Victoria and I have two different options on the table."

Claire and Harrison looked at one another, waiting for the punch line. Harlan Marks never did anything for free – especially out of the kindness of his heart. Was the hammer about to fall on a deal too good to be true?

Harlan paused to check the emotional temperature of his son and daughter-in-law. They were deeply engaged in the conversation, and their body language confirmed his observation.

"Ok," Harrison responded.

Claire nodded her head approvingly to prove she was keeping up with the conversation.

Harlan continued, "You pay only on the first note for two years. This will help reduce your mortgage payment during this time. After two years, you refinance the two notes on the house with an actual lender. At that time, Victoria and I will offer a monetary gift of $50,000 to help reduce the overall loan.

Harrison needed to walk through the plan out loud. "So, you would hold both notes for two years until we refinanced?"

"That's right."

"And we would only pay on the first note of $200,000 after a $15,000 down payment?"

"Yes," Harlan nodded.

"And with the $50,000 gift, we would pay $375,000 for a house valued at $425,000?"

"That's right," Harlan confirmed.

"Sounds good so far," Harrison chimed back while Claire nodded in agreement.

Harlan could see the light turn on in the young couples' eyes. "There's hope for these two after all," he thought.

Harrison and Claire had a ton of questions but neither one was sure what to ask. Regardless, both were too excited to put words together.

Victoria sat anxiously waiting for the younger Marks to embrace the idea. She was a bit disappointed they were able to contain their exuberance, but also impressed by their poise.

"Aren't the two initial contracts the same as a land contract agreement?" Harrison inquired.

"Not quite," Victoria finally chimed in happy to correct Harrison. "Unlike a Land Contract Agreement, the property will be immediately deeded to you."

"That's right," Harlan confirmed. "The property will truly be yours."

He had their full attention, and this pleased Harlan. He had a captive audience hanging on every word. Harrison and Claire stared at Harlan. The wheels in their head were turning to find a flaw in the proposal. Harlan knew to remain silent and let them come to their conclusion.

"You're moving to Geist Reservoir?" Claire circled back.

"It's been Harlan's dream for a long time, and we finally have the finances to make it happen," Victoria stated proudly.

Harlan Marks was a proud man. He determined he and Victoria deserved a more imposing estate after Harlan built a medical business in a matter of three short years that grew to $10 million in annual sales. The money helped make a name for themselves as they began to climb the ranks of the socialites.

Besides, they can't entertain the city's highest profile people living in a 2,000 square foot, one-story home even if it were in the community of Hidden Shores. The Marks would be frowned upon.

The Geist Reservoir setting offered multi-million dollar waterfront homes on the 1,900-acre lake in Fishers, Indiana. The sprawling paradise was home to many of the Indiana Pacers, Indianapolis Colts, and local politicians who loved the prestigious setting and had the money to spend.

Now, the 54-year-old Harlan Marks finally had the money, and he wanted to make his fortune known.

It didn't take long for them to find their $1.2 million sweeping estate. Harlan showed his impulsive behavior and purchased the property upon the first visit. The sprawling 7,200 square-foot waterfront home with outdoor gardens would suit them just fine.

Within minutes, his first order of business was to call the police and ask them to arrest the trespassing kids fishing on his property.

The second order of business was deciding what to do with the current house. The offer to his only child meant Harlan was feeling much more generous than his wife.

Claire finally broke the silence. "You said there was a second option?"

Harlan anticipated this question and was anxious to answer.

"Ha! The second option is, we don't gift any money and we stick you with the full $425,000 at refinancing." He laughed out loud but quickly realized his gaffe.

The joke was in poor taste at best and it landed with a thud. Harrison tried not to look at Victoria as he was convinced she would be the one to hatch that plan, especially if something were to happen to his father.

Regardless, Harrison and Claire realized this was a sweet deal. To pass this up would be stubborn and a slap in the face to his father. Besides, Harrison knew this wasn't Victoria's idea. Although she pretended to show excitement, he knew how she felt. It was another good reason to take her would-be profit for himself.

Harrison continued to work the deal in his head while trying to understand the motive. When it came to Harlan Marks, there was always a motive. This benefited him somehow. Was it possibly a tax break or was it to look good in front of his fake friends, many of whom had political power? Maybe this was his father's attempt to make things right for all the lost time over the past few years. Since he wasn't very good at spending time with Harrison, the next best option was to spend money on him.

The younger Marks asked for a few days to consider the offer even though mentally they were already placing furniture and hanging pictures around the room.

The evening broke up shortly after a thorough tour of the house. Harrison and Claire were sold. Harlan knew the deal was sealed.

"Why don't you go ahead and have your attorney draw up the agreement?" Harrison added. "We'll take a look at it."

The four exchanged pleasantries, while showing their appreciation for such a great opportunity.

On the way out the door, Harlan looked his son directly in the eyes. "By the way, can you give us a ride to Louisville tomorrow?"

ONE

"Of what use is money in the hand of a fool,
since he has no desire to get wisdom?"

For TWO YEARS, HARLAN'S PRIORITIES BECAME IRONCLAD. HE wanted to be among the elite of Indianapolis and his money gave him a free pass.

However, Harrison found it very disappointing and described his father as a man emotionally unprepared for the responsibility attributed to fortune and recognition.

He reminiscence about the good times with his father – riding silently on the 30-minute commute to and from Catholic military school. Yes, that's right – his best memory with his father was riding silently in a car. See, Harrison's parents decided their son needed more discipline when a third grade report card included "often rude to others." This meant Harrison was removed from public school and attended the private school run by nuns and a military sergeant.

Now, he had grown to be a responsible man. He had his moments according to Claire, but he felt grounded with respect to marriage, career, and family. He wished the same for his father but who was on wife number three, completely focused on money, and had little regard for family.

Harrison wondered if he should be more forgiving since his father helped him purchase a house that he otherwise couldn't afford. Regardless, Harrison understood all fathers set an example, whether they are good or bad.

Victoria contributed to the problem as she had no intention to nurture a relationship between her husband and his son. She already provided a house as a handsome compensation package. She considered that to be more than enough.

Together, the Marks were a small family of five and it should have been easier to gather more often than on special occasions. Harlan, like Harrison, was an only child. Harlan's elderly mother lived alone and looked forward to phone calls or visits from her son but wished for more togetherness. She said she understood everyone had a busy schedule, but the days were long without family around. Harrison spoke to Mimi often and she loved her grandson very much, but her world centered around her son. As family time goes, Mimi was about to get her wish. She was five days away from her 90th birthday.

Harrison was anticipating a call for the mandated festivities. His father called right on cue advising he and Victoria would be hosting the birthday dinner at their house this coming Saturday.

"Wonderful," Harrison thought sarcastically. "Just what I wanted to do on my Saturday evening." He and Claire were content taking his grandmother to a small diner.

"Dress accordingly," Harlan said enthusiastically to his son.

"What does that mean?" Harrison responded harshly.

"We'll be having a five-course meal Harrison, and I want you dressed for dinner and not an afternoon football game."

It was a shot at Harrison, and he knew it. If he could have reached through the phone he would have grabbed his father by the shirt collar and shook him vigorously.

"I'll wear my jeans and Butler University pull over," Harrison stated to irritate his father.

"Please, for your grandmother," Harlan said in a low pleasing voice knowing the two were close.

"This is for you and you know it. Who are we showing off to this time? Does Victoria even know how to prepare a five-course meal?" Harrison criticized.

"We'll see you at five," Harlan said sternly and hung up.

Harrison had the phone in his hand. Not one of them said goodbye.

"Ok. See you at five," Harrison said as he laughed into the phone to no one.

Getting ready Saturday night was a chore for Harrison. He quipped earlier in the week to Claire he was renting a tuxedo.

"You can wear your old prom dress," he mentioned.

"How about my wedding dress?" she chimed.

Both took the chance to laugh, silently thinking it could be the last time this evening.

They arrived at his father's scenic home and took a deep breath.

The three-level home featured majestic lake-living on an immaculate lot shaded with mature trees. It sat elegantly on the four acres of land with a coy pond situated off the back patio. The lengthy gardens loomed further in the distance. The back yard was best viewed from the terrace offering clear views of the endless reservoir. Harrison was astounded this home and view could be found in central Indiana.

Upon arrival, the large, U-shaped driveway was filled with cars. The Marks didn't recognize even one of them.

"What's is this? It's too much fanfare for Mimi's birthday dinner," Claire said pointedly.

After parking on the side of the road, Harrison and Claire reluctantly exited the car. A hollow pit turned in his stomach as he realized they had been set up. They heard sounds of laughter and conversation from inside.

Harrison glared and shook his head at Claire as she squeezed his arm to settle him down. She was just as irritated, but she needed to be the voice of reason. Claire looked over to see Harrison's forehead bright red as they navigated through the cars parked carelessly on the drive.

He reached for the door leaning in with a heavy shoulder. Immediately, the oversized cherry door opened on its own causing Harrison to fall through the opening making an unexpected grand entrance.

What he saw was shocking. He and Claire just stepped into a party that would make the Vanderbilt's blush.

The butler apologized for making the young man look foolish. Apparently, his father hired Ole' Jeeves to greet and serve each guest. The staunch old man welcomed Harrison and Claire as if he had known them for years. The tuxedo dressed gentleman ushered them into the living quarters where many distinguished couples were gathered.

The younger Marks glanced at each other momentarily sharing their surprise, if not their displeasure. They still had not wrapped their minds around their surroundings. If they didn't know better they walked into the wrong house during the wrong time era.

Harrison and Claire tried to gain their emotional footing. For the first time that day they were at least relieved they dressed appropriately, otherwise they would have been on display for all to mock.

The thick alpine beams and high ceiling were usually the focal points in the spacious home, but Claire could only cast her eyes on the people. She was even more stunned when she realized a harpist sat in the corner playing background music to the overzealous elites congesting the space.

The young Marks had visited the large house multiple times before. The heavy wooden bookcase and imported fireplace from Deggendorf, Germany were always impressive but now they couldn't get past the candelabra's adding to the lavishness.

Everyone was talking to one another at the same time. The room was obnoxious since each guest wanted to be heard rather than carry an intelligent conversation.

A waiter soon approached and offered wine in a choice of red or white. Grabbing one of each, Harrison asked the waiter, "Where is Harlan Marks?"

"I'm afraid Mr. Marks isn't here yet, Sir. May I ask the butler to inform you upon his arrival?"

"He's not here? Where the hell is he?" Harrison was fed up and had seen enough as he continued to scan the room for familiar faces.

"He went to pick up his mother for her party," the butler explained as he stepped in to relieve the waiter of the awkward exchange. "He'll return momentarily; I'm sure."

Harrison wanted to leave but couldn't bring himself to walk out the door. Everything was over the top, even for Victoria and Harlan.

As the two found an open corner, Harrison began to recognize faces.

"That's the Indianapolis Mayor and his wife," he pointed out to Claire. "Are you kidding me?"

Harrison may have considered starting a conversation with the mayor, but since he enjoyed sticking his hands into the taxpayer's pockets, Harrison thought otherwise.

"And there's the commodore of the Indianapolis Yacht Club," Claire whispered.

They had met the commodore and his wife on a previous encounter at the Murat Centre. Claire landed tickets from her boss last December for the Nutcracker in the private balcony. She and Harrison sat directly next to the distinguished couple and enjoyed their company. Harrison fell asleep during the performance and Claire still hadn't forgiven him.

The room was filled with bankers and business owners including photographers from the newspaper.

"What are we doing here?" Harrison asked as he shook his head in disgust.

"Better yet, what are they all doing here?" Claire questioned as she looked around a room of elites.

Harrison found an uncongested area by the back window and threw back his third glass of wine. His father came up from behind and subtly spoke in Harrison's ear.

"What do you think?"

Harrison glanced at his watch and then at Claire. "I think it's time for me to leave. I was supposed to attend my grandmother's birthday party with my family. I'm afraid I'm at the wrong house."

Harrison was callous in his response, but his father walked away unphased and eager to greet the pretentious guests.

Mimi emerged from the maze of people hoping to find solace among her grandson and his wife. At 4' 11" and 90 pounds she was too small to see over anyone. She spoke slowly while her eyes moved feverishly around the room.

"This is all too much for my birthday," she insisted to Claire in a whisper as she bowed and shook her head.

She recoiled her tiny body behind Harrison as if she were about to be run down by a careless group of concert goers.

Claire didn't have the heart to tell her the party wasn't for her at all. It was just made to look that way. The three of them were merely invited to take part only to witness the lavish lifestyle the elder Marks now enjoyed.

At some point in the fiasco, Harlan stopped the party to say a few words about his mother's birthday. The guests thought he was a sweet man for speaking from the heart. His mother was slightly grateful but disappointed she couldn't spend quality time with the few people she loved.

Victoria, on the other hand, used the number of people as a barrier to avoid conversation with her three family members. She glanced only so often making polite eye contact but never came over to speak.

"I think she's still angry because I didn't appreciate her Christmas gift," Harrison laughed.

"Well, how did she expect us to respond after she gave you a half used candle?" Claire asked. "Of course we're going to laugh."

"I still can't believe it," Mimi mocked. "She just wanted to get rid of it because she didn't like the scent."

They all shook their heads in disbelief over Victoria's impropriety.

Two hours was all Harrison could handle. He hated to leave his grandmother alone with these opportunists, but he had seen enough. After downing his sixth glass of wine, he grabbed Claire by the hand and said annoyingly, "Let's get the hell out of here."

Claire was more than willing. During the party, she strategically found a corner of the room to avoid the chaos and dirty old men from grabbing her from behind.

They said goodbye to his grandmother. Harrison and Claire left nearly unnoticed except for the butler still tending the door. They didn't even bother to inform his father.

Only small talk ensued between the young couple as they drove away. Neither one of them really cared to talk given their disgust for what they just experienced. Unfortunately, something needed to be said.

"It's more important for them to be A-Lister's than to spend time with family," Harrison mumbled to Claire.

"I'm sorry it's like this," she sympathized not knowing what else to say.

"He's heading for regret. It's all about the show," he said. "He's just so damn arrogant."

"Maybe the distance between the two of you is for the best? For now, anyway...," Claire said as she tried to make sense of it all. "I feel most sorry for your grandmother."

It was a foregone conclusion that his father was losing focus on the people that mattered. Unfortunately, it was the life his father chose which made the situation even worse.

Claire usually kept silent regarding Harrison's father as it didn't often affect her husband's well-being, but that was now being challenged. She checked in with him occasionally while lying in bed, but he didn't like her to know when he was upset. At times, Claire would slip and let her feelings about his father be known. Those instances stung Harrison to the core. Even then, Claire wasn't as critical as she desired.

TWO

*"He who pursues righteousness and love finds life,
prosperity and honor."*

HARRISON AND CLAIRE MET AT BUTLER UNIVERSITY SIX YEARS EARLIER
in a communication theory class.

Claire entered college knowing that she wanted to major in the same
subject and eventually pursue a master's degree. Teaching at a large university
was not out of the question for the ambitious honors student, as long as it
meant getting out of her small hometown in Madison, Indiana.

Harrison started college one year earlier. Unfortunately, he was no further ahead than Claire. Currently enrolled as *undecided*, he was desperate to
find something he liked. Short stints pursuing Economics and Accounting
proved futile once Harrison realized he was not good at math. His mother
was growing impatient.

Now remarried, Harrison's mother, Joanne, was determined to provide
a college education for her only child. It was an opportunity she wanted for
him since she was not given the chance to attend college. She was a skilled
secretary and could type 135 words per minute. Although now in her early
fifties, she stayed on top of the ever-changing technology. Joanne continued
to apply for secretarial positions at the university years earlier, knowing that
her son wanted to pursue higher education. She was also aware that she could
not afford to send her son to school on a secretary's salary. She finally landed
a position at the university's Human Resource Department, and now her son
would attend school free of charge.

Harrison enrolled in his fifth communication class toward the end of his third year of college. He discovered that he was a natural at public speaking and writing after taking a Communication 100-level course one year earlier. Another easy class would buy him the additional time he needed before declaring a major.

He didn't notice Claire initially. She kept to herself, and he was always surrounded by friends. Although he lacked much-needed academic motivation, his social agenda proved ambitious. Fraternity parties and extended stays at the surrounding bars made him a familiar face with students.

From Harrison's perspective, it wasn't *who you know* but *who knows you*, and this often worked to his advantage. When he needed quick answers for a homework grade, a willing acquaintance always came through. He never considered himself cheating. He looked at it as being resourceful.

Halfway through the semester, Claire caught his eye. Since she always sat in the front of the class, it was no wonder she went unnoticed. She was quietly stunning with her long brown hair and thin frame. A simple smile from Harrison caused her cheeks to redden and look away. He knew right away this girl was humble yet sophisticated. He also knew she was out of his league. No matter, he would say hello. It certainly wouldn't hurt to meet one more person, especially if she was a member of the opposite sex.

"So it's an interesting class," Harrison mentioned to the pretty co-ed as he timed his exit from class perfectly.

"It's been fun so far," she smiled back as if she had known him for years. Claire was intrigued by Harrison from the beginning. She found herself trying to catch glimpses of him and wondered if he would ever take interest. The studious girl conveniently turned around when students from the back room would ask Dr. Fisher questions. She would admit that he was attractive, but she was too proper to fall for his overrated charm.

"Dr. Fisher seems to like you. He calls on you a lot during class", Harrison said as they walked down the stairs together. It was a clumsy comment, and

Harrison knew it. Unfortunately, he had to force conversation as he wasn't sure how much time he had before she split in another direction.

"He's my advisor, so I know him fairly well," Claire stated.

"Oh, I see. So where are you from?" he stumbled, trying to keep the conversation going.

"It's a small town. I guarantee you never heard of it."

"Try me. I'm pretty good with geography."

"Well, have you heard of Madison?" she asked, knowing his answer in advance.

"Nope", Harrison admitted. Better to admit defeat now than pretend he knew the town's whereabouts. She seemed too intelligent to fool.

It didn't take a communication major to figure out that Harrison was flirting with her. Claire found it amusing but was cautious. She had just ended a long-term relationship and wasn't in a hurry to resume the dating scene. On the contrary, she didn't have male friends and thought it wouldn't hurt to be kind.

This escapade went on for the remainder of the semester. Harrison walked with her toward her dorm before peeling away a few minutes before, stating his car was nearby. Actually, his car was parked on the opposite side of campus. He wanted to maximize as much time with Claire as possible. Often, he was tempted to walk her back to her dorm, but he didn't want to appear creepy. Most of the way would have to do for now.

Besides, they always took the long way back, taking advantage of the winding sidewalks past the Holcomb Observatory that headed north toward the lake. Historic Hinkle Fieldhouse stood in the distance, and Harrison would say goodbye. All in all, if Harrison managed the trip properly, it allowed for nearly 20 minutes of conversation.

On the last day of class, lightning struck. Dr. Fisher mentioned that he was looking for lab assistants next fall. The lucky hires would help him teach his Communication 100-level course and get exposure to the other professors within the department. It was a job that paid little but looked good on a resume, according to the professor. Harrison wasn't interested at first since Dr. Fisher said that applicants must be a communication major.

After the class was dismissed, Claire waited in the hall, expecting Harrison would join her for their final walk on a beautiful May afternoon. He hurried to say goodbye to friends then headed toward the beautiful 21-year-old. It was a crapshoot if they would ever have another class together, so he wasn't going to risk losing this last opportunity.

"Are you thinking of teaching with Dr. Fisher next fall?" Claire immediately inquired, hoping Harrison was a candidate.

"I'm thinking about it," he lied, trying to recall what she was referencing. "What about you?"

"Yep. I've already submitted my application," she said proudly.

Their walk now turned into a slow shuffle as the two wanted to make it last as long as possible. Harrison allowed Claire to talk the rest of the way back to her dorm. He couldn't focus on anything she was saying. He had to spend more time with her, and it was clear the only way to do it was to teach that class.

Walking shoulder to shoulder, Harrison silently declared Communication as his major. He had to talk to Dr. Fisher immediately.

"Well, I guess I'll see you in three months," Claire said, hoping it was true.

"I know you will," Harrison said confidently as if he knew something she didn't.

He did know something. He had just taken a big step in his career path based on a girl. He had no clue what he could do with a communication degree, but that didn't matter. His mother would be relieved that her son finally became serious about his future. She didn't need to know the reasoning behind his decision.

He hugged Claire. It was the first hug they would ever share. He smiled one last time, then turned and walked away. Under different circumstances, he would have stayed longer. He would have asked stupid questions about her plans for the summer, something Claire had already shared with him 10 minutes earlier, but he wasn't listening.

"Take care!" he shouted as he grew further away. "The next couple of months will go by quickly!" This was Harrison's encouragement to her and everyone within a 100-yard earshot.

When Harrison thought he was out of sight, he went into a full-blown sprint toward Dr. Fisher's office. He found the professor at his desk, preparing to leave. He knocked abruptly on the already-open door.

"Dr. Fisher, I would like to declare my major, and I would like you to be my advisor," Harrison said with enthusiasm.

Dr. Fisher was initially shocked by the abrupt statement but more than pleased with Harrison's decision. He had Harrison three times in class and thought highly of him. Harrison earned an A in the first two classes, and he was about to earn another.

"I also want to apply for one of the open lab assistant positions if you will allow?" he uttered in desperation. If he didn't get the position, his objective of pursuing a major in this field would be meaningless. It seemed like forever for Dr. Fisher to decide. Harrison's love life now hinged upon his reply. The perfect plan, hatched only moments ago, could crash down, and it was entirely out of Harrison's control.

"I would be happy to interview you. I'm scheduling interviews this week," the professor proclaimed while winking at Harrison.

Harrison then scheduled a private meeting with one of his acquaintances, who was already a lab teacher for the professor. Two days later, Harrison sat with Dr. Fisher and nailed the interview. He would be a lab assistant with Claire in a few short months.

Upon hanging up after the call, Harrison dropped into his chair and buried his head into his hands. He was overwhelmed with gratitude.

"Thank you, Jesus. Thank you, Jesus!" he proclaimed over and over again.

Maybe it was time to consider his faith more seriously.

There's plenty of time for that, he thought.

The lab assistants returned two weeks before the fall semester. Claire was elated to see that she was going to spend more time with her new friend.

Soon she was calling Harrison in the evening to compare notes. Only minutes into the conversation, they were sharing personal stories that lasted well into the night. Harrison was in love.

Claire was now living in an apartment off-campus when Harrison showed up at her doorstep. She was surprised to see him.

"Get your shoes, and let's go," he told her.

"What? Where are we going?"

"You'll find out. Let's go."

Claire didn't like surprises, but she liked Harrison. She wasn't going to turn him down. He politely but firmly grabbed her by the arm and escorted her down the stairs into his car. Claire was still confused, but she knew something fun was about to happen. He had a mischievous look about him, and she liked it.

"I only take important people to this place," Harrison said, assessing Claire's mood. She was wondering what she got herself into with this so-called friend and his over-confident bullishness. Harrison saw through that, however. He knew she was anxious to find out where they were going, and she couldn't hide it.

"What if I had something planned tonight?" Claire questioned with a bit of attitude. "You may have just interrupted my evening."

"Ha! You? Something going on tonight?" Harrison mocked. "Sorting your sock drawer again?"

They both laughed. Soon, Harrison and Claire arrived at Shapiro's Delicatessen. It was a tasty sandwich café serving the city of Indianapolis since 1940. The place was like stepping back in time. It was slightly remodeled in 2002 to keep with city code, but the decor wasn't what brought folks into the best-kept secret in the city.

"You like pie?" Harrison asked, opening the door to the throwback establishment.

"Maybe?" Claire said flirtatiously. "But what if I don't?"

"You will after this," Harrison declared.

Harrison and Claire sat down for their first date. If this girl didn't fall in love with him after tasting the best scutterbotch pie in the world, it was time to walk away. Yes, scutterbotch!

By mid-October, they were officially dating. Harrison felt relief after an anxiety-filled summer. He was able to cross the final task off his relationship checklist that made Claire his girl. He had executed his master plan perfectly over the last few months. Before long, they were talking about marriage and family once they set graduation dates and career paths.

Claire loved telling the story of how they met to friends, family, and anyone who would listen. When Harrison was present during the story he denied the truth and told a different version. According to him, Claire's car broke down on the side of a country road in the middle of a rainstorm. He came along and got the car restarted while getting soaked and nearly catching pneumonia and nearly dying. She nursed him back to health, waiting on his fever to break for weeks. Harrison found this narration more appealing as it made him seem less desperate than the truth.

Claire rolled her eyes behind his back each time he told the story. Anyone who knew Harrison immediately realized it wasn't true because he couldn't fix anything on a car or otherwise.

Claire took Harrison to Madison often during their courtship. She loved to spend time with her parents, and she was proud to have Harrison escort her to church on Sundays. He grew fond of Trinity United Methodist Church and felt a sense of comfort. Perhaps it was another step for him in his faith journey. Whatever it was, he had a long way to go.

They both graduated at the same time, although Harrison was on a five-year plan. The engagement came quickly and so did Claire's first job offer.

She babysat for friends of her parents during college summers in Carmel, Indiana, an Indianapolis suburb. It also allowed her to remain close to Harrison.

Claire referred to the two boys lovingly as Lucifer and Beelzebub. It was agreed upon between the boys' father and Claire that he would introduce her to his best friend Trent Sutton if she would babysit during the summer months.

Sutton owned a manufacturing company that made steel framed tables and chairs. His Indianapolis-based mega-corporation held contracts with high-profile companies, including hotel chains and two NFL teams. He was looking for a young, attractive woman with the ability to speak in front of large groups and sell his products.

He found what he was looking for in Claire. Sutton knew Claire wanted to eventually work in human resources for the company, which employed over 300 people. After only a few months, Claire got her break.

The $42,000 offer was a far cry from Claire's insistence that she be compensated no less than $67,900 so she could stay in the Indianapolis area. It was a line-in-the-sand statement Harrison never let her live down.

"$67,900?" he would ask jokingly. "Couldn't you bother to round up?"

It wasn't much of a secret that Harrison was able to make up the $15,900 shortfall. With an engagement ring on her finger that Claire wasn't about to give back, she accepted the job offer.

Harrison's career path was more challenging and entertaining to share with friends.

Three months after graduation, Harrison landed a job as general manager at a commissary. It paid the bills for a year and helped the couple through their nuptials. However, after only 14 months there, the company closed. It was just as well, as he came home smelling of grease daily.

Fortunately for the young couple, they were able to take advantage of friendships to help Harrison find his next job. The bright and beautiful phenom at Sutton Manufacturing also made a close work friend. The friendship developed, and the ladies decided to bring the husbands into the mix and have an evening together. Hockey games and dinners became a common theme for the two couples.

One Saturday evening, Kyle and Corrine Mitchell invited the Marks' for dinner. This time it involved taking the Mitchell's boat on the Geist Reservoir to Bella Vita's. The two couples returned to the house on the bank of the reservoir. Kyle's parents owned the home and called it their permanent home. It was a 4,000-square-foot condo overlooking The Geist.

After a house tour with cocktails in hand, the couple took their seat on the porch situated on the river's steep hillside. The deck was the perfect viewpoint as it stared down the 75-foot-bank to the brisk, steel-blue water.

After multiple alcoholic drinks enjoying the sunset, Kyle's parents came home and joined them for a nightcap.

Trying to be polite, Harrison stood up from the chaise lounge chair and offered his seat.

"Please sit down," he said to the lady.

Hell, it's her chair anyway, he thought.

The thought startled him as he took quick inventory to ensure that he didn't say that out loud. After the second Tom Collins with double shots of gin, he was a little sketchy with internal conversations versus the spoken words that required a filter. He would have used her name when he offered the seat, but the gin erased her name from his memory.

Keeping his poise, he picked up a short stool and prepared to place it on the deck. As he sat, he didn't notice that the back leg was not on the deck. In one of his most undignified moments, Harrison unwittingly did a backflip off the deck's edge into the bushes five feet below. If that wasn't enough, the bank leading to the river was so steep that he continued to tumble backward and gain speed toward the water. He came to rest 20-feet later against a tree and remained still to make sure he didn't break any bones.

After the brief diagnosis of his 6 foot 2 inches and 205-pound-frame, Harrison determined he was okay. He also came to realize that everyone on the deck was laughing. Making light of the situation, Harrison laughed out loud. He was thankful that he was not hurt while his laughing covered up his severely damaged ego.

Harrison and Claire had no idea how important that encounter with the Mitchell's would impact their future.

Two months later Harrison's company announced a plant closure that began immediately. Now out of work, newly married, and living in a house that was slightly outside of their budget, it was time to call on those who were well connected.

Claire suggested that he call Kyle's father. The elder man was Vice President of a large company in Indianapolis. At the very least, he could be a reference.

Harrison placed a call to Evergreen Paper Company the next day and asked to speak with Mr. John Mitchell. The secretary put him through to Harrison's surprise.

"Hello, John Mitchell," said the gruff voice on the other end.

"Hello, Mr. Mitchell, my name is Harrison Marks, and I am friends with…"

"Are you the same Harrison Marks that fell off my porch?" the voice on the other end interrupted.

Trying hard to contain a laugh and feeling a sense of relief, Harrison responded, "Yes, Sir. That's me."

After a brief explanation of why he made the call, John invited Harrison to stop in for a discussion the following week.

He was hired a month later as a sales representative, selling empty boxes to manufacturing companies throughout Indiana. As an international company with deep pockets, Harrison was now working in a profession that he could call a career.

Life was back on track for the young couple as they had planned.

Maybe Harrison's father had been right about a sales profession all along.

THREE

"A fool finds no pleasure in understanding
but delights in airing his own opinions."

HARLAN GROANED AS HE AND VICTORIA, PULLED INTO THE Downtown Marriott valet. He pretended to be annoyed but deep down this is what he wanted all along. He had arrived physically and financially, and it was important to him that others knew it on both accounts.

"Are you nervous?" Victoria asked as Harlan shifted the Jaguar into park.

Her husband of four years was asked by the Indianapolis Area Small Business Association, in connection with the Indianapolis Chamber of Commerce, to be the keynote speaker for the 12th Annual Indianapolis Small Business Association Banquet about growing local business.

"If only Indy Entrepreneur Magazine could see me now," he joked.

Three months ago, much to Harlan's amusement, the monthly issue listed him as one of Indianapolis' top 10 small business owners. The top 10 owners were judged on taking personal risk, investment in the community, job creation, and overall, making the city a more vibrant place to live. It was a welcomed honor that created much chatter among the small business community, especially with the local real estate investors.

Harlan Marks was riding a financial wave. In a matter of five short years he built a medical business that grew to $10 million in annual sales. He parlayed the income into becoming one of the largest private real estate investors in the Indianapolis market owning condominiums and apartment complexes recently valued at $41 million.

The climb to prestige was exceptional and Harlan estimated that 10 percent of the 500 dinner tickets sold were other real estate investors who were furious he broke on to the scene without their permission. He wasn't invited into their fraternity but now there was nothing they could do to keep him out.

Anyone who was anyone was expected to be at the event. If the attendees didn't care for Harlan, they were at least present to be seen with the most influential and well-to-do people in the Indianapolis area.

It was important for Harlan to arrive on time, but not too early. He was the featured speaker and would be sitting on the elevated stage for all to see. When he walked into the ballroom many people turned to look. Familiar and unfamiliar faces corralled to greet him, and Harlan relished the moment. Victoria, standing and clutching his arm, smiled admirably at her hero. She knew this was her moment too. She wasn't giving a speech, but those who knew the power couple understood she was an integral part of the business success.

Now at the age of 56, she accepted the accolades with great reverence. Fame was the next best thing to money and Harlan acquired both. Victoria was content with just the money, but she knew what this meant to her husband.

The courtesy handshakes and polite conversations were tedious. Neither one was comfortable around people they didn't know, but they weren't about to flinch. Besides, they didn't have to do anything other than smile and pretend to care. Soon the elder Marks were settled, and guests were forced to take their seat far away from the table of honor. They were on display for all to see.

Commodore Gerald P. Rapp, a close friend of the Marks from the Indianapolis Yacht Club, took his position at the podium. Noticing it was time to start the festivities, the groups broke up and found their designated table.

Commodore Rapp began, "Could you all bow your heads for grace?" It was more of a command than a question.

Harlan rolled his eyes not remembering he was seated where every gaze was upon him.

Is this necessary? he thought with obvious annoyance.

He didn't grow up in the church, didn't believe in God, and had no use for something intangible such as religion. It was fool's gold, according to Harlan. The harder he worked, the luckier he became. His success was based entirely on his own doing and not the blessing of an imperial ghost. Jesus and God were fairy-tale creatures for people who were weak and couldn't take care of themselves.

Victoria bowed her head in the meantime. She was more familiar with the concept given her Catholic upbringing, but she had enough church in her earlier years to last a lifetime. She bowed her head for posterity purposes only.

Life was going so well for the Marks. They didn't need a god at this point in their lives, nor would they have time for one if they desired. As far as the Marks were concerned, cash was king and nothing else.

The prayer was over before Harlan could finish his internal bashing of Christianity. He never heard a word of Commodore Rapp's blessing. "Let's eat" was about as much of an "Amen" as Harlan was going to give.

After an elegant meal, the introduction began.

"Ladies and gentlemen," the hostess had announced to a full audience. "Our guest tonight needs little introduction. He is the business owner of Marks Medical Supply that originally started in his one-car garage here in Indianapolis, Indiana. Today, this once one-man operation has become a standalone building with a vice-president of operations, a receptionist, dedicated salespeople, purchasing and accounting departments, customer service, and a shipping department – totaling 45 employees in all."

Harlan got lost in the introduction and reflected briefly on his journey. Five years earlier, he discovered through the care of his 85-year-old mother that medical supplies for the elderly could be well compensated. After all, it became quite expensive to care for those who couldn't fully care for themselves. He began purchasing creams, lotions, gauze, tape, and even adult diapers in bulk before he realized these things were all reimbursed through Medicare as long as the elderly individual qualified. If he could put together kits and other packages needed by area nursing home patients, he could build a small business for himself that was sustainable.

The hostess continued. "It was during this time Harlan and his lovely wife Victoria realized with great success comes great responsibility."

"Where is she going with this?" Harlan whispered to Victoria.

Victoria didn't hear a word of what Harlan said as she was too enamored with the introduction that made them even more adored. She felt pity for those who couldn't experience her life. The vacations, the jewelry, the clothes, finer restaurants, and imported cars were just a few things she now considered necessities.

"The urge to do more for their community got the best of them when they realized our great city needed affordable quality housing for many middle-class residents. The Marks used the profits from their medical business and began investing in area condominiums and apartment complexes in Indianapolis."

Applause rang out again as Harlan whispered under his breath, "If it's so affordable, maybe we should raise the rates."

Victoria heard her husband and gave him nudge a under the table. Although she agreed with his assessment, this was not the time nor the place for the conversation. She knew the guests were scrutinizing their every move and reaction.

The truth is, it didn't take long before Harlan's ego and Victoria's demand for better things got the best of them. The real estate market created another avenue for wealth and one with less government oversight. He needed to diversify his portfolio, and the Marks knew the right people to make it happen. While many of the attendees took the introduction as truth, many of Harlan's real estate foes agreed this was giving the Marks too much credit. They didn't appreciate this couple that rose to the top in such a short time.

"You may have seen Mr. Marks recognized in our Indy Entrepreneur Magazine," she went on and the crowd began to nod enthusiastically.

She began reading excerpts out of the article that even made Harlan blush. What seemed like forever, the woman appeared to show no signs of relinquishing the microphone.

After one final applause, it was Harlan Marks' turn to speak.

Harlan stood awkwardly and made his way to the podium. He was a man that loved to hear himself speak and took pride in his ability to command a room with his confidence if not his arrogance. He found himself weak at the knees as the guest all stared back at him. It couldn't have been the wine because he left the glass untouched fearing he would lose his edge. For whatever reason, he realized he loved to talk, but maybe he wasn't a great speaker. His ego didn't agree, and he charged on.

The small-framed 5 foot 8 inch man with thinning hair never bothered to thank the hostess for the introduction. It wasn't because he ignored the common courtesy, but because he forgot about public speaking protocol. He was a self-serving individual that placed himself in the center. If he displayed an act of kindness, it was because it served himself, and it was just a coincidence someone else benefited in the process.

The evening finished with all the attendees showing their appreciation for the Marks. Although the couple was exhausted, they still managed to spend quality time saying goodbye to the significant people.

A group of real estate entrepreneurs huddled in the back. They couldn't wait to discuss the problems Harlan Marks created once he infiltrated their exclusive group. It didn't go unnoticed by Harlan and Victoria. Honestly, they found it very amusing. The two realized very early that success came with a price, and losing a few fake friends was a small price to pay. Friends were an evil necessity anyway. Friends are important to have for these occasions, but they seemed to require too much effort to maintain. Harlan knew he couldn't have one without the other.

It was time to put this evening to bed. As Harlan prepared to open the car door for his wife, his phone rang. He already dismissed a call from his son moments ago and sent the call to voice mail. He suspected this was Harrison's second attempt.

Harlan took the phone out of his blazer. He looked at his caller ID before he ignored the call again. He was wrapping up an important night and he wanted to relish the moment without distraction. He realized it was someone other than whom he thought. He knew he had to take the call.

"Just a moment, Victoria – this shouldn't take long," he stated disdainfully.

Harlan glanced at his watch. It was 9:30 p.m.

As if talking to his phone, he then questioned aloud, "What is so important he has to call on a Wednesday night?"

Harlan Marks was never out of reach when it came to his business and tonight would be no exception. It wasn't uncommon for attorneys, realtors, bankers, or his company's vice president to contact him late at night.

Victoria recognized the frustration on her husband's face, and she suspected she knew the reason for the call. Although Harlan tried to take the call in private by stepping away from his wife, she continued to listen carefully.

"Harlan Marks," he answered abruptly as always. His voice was intimidating for a man of his small stature.

After a short pause, Harlan spoke again. "Tell me now."

Victoria couldn't hear the entire conversation, but not for lack of trying. For Jay Hausmann to call, she recognized the significance.

"That's not what we discussed, Jay," Harlan said with authority.

Victoria knew this wasn't good, and she stopped listening to the remainder of the conversation. Her husband didn't respond well to bad news, and she didn't want to be around for it.

Although Harlan wasn't talking, he wasn't listening either. He was only waiting for the voice on the other end to finish.

"This is what I recall from our conversation, Jay. They don't have the resources, and this is embarrassing to them."

Another long pause caused Harlan to grow impatient. "We are not taking the deal. Get it done." Harlan Marks hung up the phone without saying goodbye.

Harlan handed a $20 tip to the valet. He was so angry he couldn't remember to open the door for Victoria, who had become accustomed to her husband's chivalry. She quickly got in and closed the door. There was no sense in standing outside the car to prove a point. Besides, he may have driven off without her and not even noticed.

Harlan started the car and emotionally distanced himself. It was a shield he placed around himself when he needed time to solve a problem that he wasn't ready to discuss. Victoria learned early in their relationship to give her husband the space and time he needed to resolve his matters. In time, she would hear the details. To enter his no-fly-zone prematurely would result in an unwelcome argument. She let ten minutes go by on a silent ride home before she proceeded with the line of questioning.

"Are you sure this is the right thing to do?" she asked.

Victoria knew the answer she was going to get before she even spoke. She wasn't willing to wait this one out. It was the only strategy to get him to talk.

Among Harlan's many hot buttons, being second guessed ranked with the best of them.

"Yes," was all he was willing to say.

He would be better in the morning and potentially have the solution in mind, but now he needed time. The ride home remained quiet. Victoria placed her hand around her husband's neck to help ease the tension. It was too late. An evening of fun and praise just ended with a thud.

FOUR

"A wife of noble character, who can find?
She is worth far more than rubies."

HARRISON EXITED THE EXPRESSWAY HEADING TOWARD HIS LAKEFRONT home after a busy week at work. Hours of driving and visiting customers made for an honest day of work. Daily road trips were frequent in his line of business, but it was Friday afternoon for a salesperson on a beautiful 80 degrees spring day.

He turned onto 86th Street and noticed the dry cleaner on the left. Harrison remembered an armful of clothes that he dropped off a week earlier but now it would have to wait. As he crossed the intersection heading toward the overpass, the Methodist church steeple approached in the distance. He drove past it every day on the way home.

Blessed are the meek, for they shall inherit the earth, today's outdoor bulletin read. Harrison recognized the scripture from a sermon a few months ago when he and Claire attended church with her parents in Madison. Pastor Bob did a great job breaking down the Beatitudes from Jesus' Sermon on the Mount. He started to feel guilty for not being a regular churchgoer. He only attended church if he and Claire spent the weekend with her parents. He let the guilt pass quickly. Life seemed just fine. Besides, he was eager to get home.

He cruised slowly through Hidden Shores, enjoying the peaceful accompaniment of chirping birds and sunlight bursting through the trees. The lake water reflected the sun like flashbulbs into an unsuspecting eye. It all contributed to the brilliance of the afternoon.

Harrison offered a courtesy wave and smiled at those taking a walk or tending to their lawn. It was a small price to pay for his sanctuary waiting around the bend.

Adding to his enthusiasm, he met with a travel agent during his lunch break. It was an unintended appointment, but his impulsive personality got the best of him. Harrison and Claire often talked about a two-week tour of Europe, so he seized the opportunity to speak with an agent. For no reason, he decided this was the day he and Claire would commit to the trip. His enthusiasm could sometimes be contagious. He hoped it was enough to convince his wife.

The previous Indiana winter dumped feet of snow with brutally cold temperatures still causing Harrison to shiver. Flatland bordered the Midwest city on all four sides. Cold fronts and the wind gained momentum swirling down from Canada and the Great Lakes. The winter weather only added to the discomfort provoking everyone to ask why they lived in such a volatile climate.

It was time to pull the trigger on this vacation.

The sparkling lake should have caught his eye first as he entered the house, but the 18-month-old pug demanded attention. Zoe twisted and spun to her choreography for anyone who entered the family home. The view would have to wait until he scratched her ears and rubbed her belly.

Harrison retreated to the master bedroom closet. He changed into his swimsuit and raggedy Butler University T-shirt that Claire had thrown away at least a dozen times. He walked with childlike excitement for the patio door to take advantage of the spectacular lake.

"Come on Zoe!" Harrison said excitedly.

He slapped the side of his leg, and Zoe sprinted across the living room. It didn't take much to get her fired up. Her youthful enthusiasm caused her to forget she needed to pace herself on the solid wood surface, and she slid into the kitchen table. Despite his embarrassment for the little pet, she was family. He couldn't turn down her need for companionship and boat rides.

The two made their way off the patio that extended the length of the house. Stepping onto the lawn, Harrison tried harder than Zoe to navigate the goose droppings in the backyard before leaping toward the boat dock. He turned around and scooped up the 15 lb. dog knowing she would somehow find her way into the water – even though she couldn't swim. There was a reason this silly little animal was the last pup remaining in a litter of five.

He stepped foot onto the 18-foot boat, and the glass reflection on the water immediately shattered. As the boat pulled away from the dock, Harrison and Zoe both looked up and breathed in the fresh air. Moments later, Harrison brought the boat to a slow drift as the pontoon softly skidded to a halt upon the shallow sandbar.

Harrison stretched out along the back of the boat. He couldn't wait for his wife to arrive home to share his news.

Harrison even considered making his famous *yellow dinner* if it would help put a smile on Claire's face. She coined the name when she came home late one evening to have an all-yellow plate of food sitting at a candle-lit dining room table. She appreciated the gesture but more than that, she had a great story to tell her co-workers anytime Harrison found the urge to please his wife's palate. Grilled cheese, chicken noodle soup, and corn was the chef's choice when he gave Claire a break from the kitchen.

Harrison thought they would travel in October to celebrate their third wedding anniversary. First, he had to study the material to ensure he knew the information thoroughly.

Claire would try to shoot down the idea. She was the type of person that would want to go, but her practicality often interfered with her husband's brilliant ideas.

I can't allow her to say, 'No' this time. What wife could turn down a trip to Europe?

France, Spain, and Germany were among the places he wanted to visit. With only two weeks to travel, they needed to narrow the choices. A second European trip would follow to visit Belgium, Switzerland, and The Netherlands. Italy would be a separate trip altogether.

Maybe it was the slight rocking of the boat or the sun's rays that allowed Harrison to relax. Regardless, he was somewhere between meditation and blissful slumber when he was jolted awake by the sound of someone screaming his name. Pulling himself together, Harrison looked to the shore. Standing on his boat dock was a tall brunette with high heels and a flowing dress. Her beauty was enough to capture anyone's attention, as long as they weren't in the middle of an afternoon nap.

Zoe recognized the voice and started with her joyful antics once again. Harrison smiled and waved at Claire from afar.

He sensed the excitement in her voice, and he proceeded with the three-minute boat ride back to shore. Claire never took her eyes off her husband. The closer he came, the more her smile radiated. Harrison greeted her nervously as he knew it was time for his presentation. Claire was going to be his most difficult customer of the week. He prayed he could close the deal.

"Good afternoon, beautiful," he said as he arrived at the dock. "May I interest you in a ride with the captain? I promise not to tell your husband, as I assume you're a married woman."

Harrison was quick and playful, especially when causing his bride to blush. The game didn't last long once Claire recognized the tattered Butler T-shirt that somehow made its way out of the garbage. Harrison realized her displeasure right away.

"What was I thinking?" Harrison reprimanded himself out loud as he looked down at his shirt. He was half-serious while making light of a slight mishap in judgment.

Claire brushed off the indignant shirt and returned to character. She extended her hand in continental fashion for Harrison to assist her coming aboard.

"Why, certainly. How could a girl resist such a temptation?" she flirted. "My husband won't mind. I'm sure he's watching a silly sport on television. He'll never know we're gone."

Harrison ignored the slight. He deserved it. Basketball was his mistress but that was a winter sport. He was just glad the focus was now off his T-shirt. Anyway, he had a more pressing topic to reveal.

Harrison unveiled his serious side. "I have something to share with you Claire. You're going to love it!"

He directed the boat back to the sandbar. The master plan was coming together, and Claire was still an unsuspecting participant.

"I can't wait," she beamed. "I have something to share with you too."

Harrison brought the boat to a halt again upon the soft sand. Claire was still partially occupied by the over-zealous dog who was threatening to snag her silk sun dress.

He reached for the brochures that he had hidden from his wife.

"We've been waiting to do this for three years," he began.

He handed her a stack of brochures, abandoning his well-planned strategy.

"Our bank account is solid, and we continue to put your entire income into savings each month," he continued. "We'll get to see Paris, Barcelona, Hamburg and all the other cities in Europe on a two-week, once in a lifetime, vacation."

Claire's eyes glazed over just as Harrison knew would happen. He went unfazed and went back to his script as best he could.

"I think we should…"

"Stop. Just stop, Harrison. STOP, STOP," she had to shout.

She sighed at the extra effort required to get his attention – this was not uncommon. When Harrison had center stage, it was difficult to steal the spotlight. Claire was appreciative of her husband's intention. She knew the trip was something they both wanted.

Harrison sat confused as she handed him a gift bag. He didn't know why he hadn't noticed it before.

The bag was not masculine, which provoked a suspicious look toward Claire. He stared at the bag and back again at his wife. She nodded encouragingly and shook the bag in front of his face.

"Go ahead. It's yours to open," she nearly whispered.

Now Claire was smiling, and she appeared in complete control of the conversation.

Still focused on his agenda, Harrison was disturbed Claire could place more importance on a silly bag. His fabulous proposal appeared in jeopardy. Even more frustrating, he didn't prepare for an interruption.

Bewildered, Harrison reached into the gift bag and pulled out a cloth. He held it in one hand and looked skeptically at his wife.

"A washcloth?" he asked in confusion.

"Oh my God! Do I have to do everything for you? Read what it says!"

Harrison examined the item more closely.

It read, "I Love My Daddy."

He realized it wasn't a washcloth. It was a baby's bib. He looked back at Claire, who was now enjoying her husband's discovery. It took another moment to grasp. His eyes widened, and his frustration turned to joy.

Europe would have to wait. The young couple would be expecting their first child in December.

FIVE

"Even a child is known by his actions,
by whether his conduct is pure and right."

IT WASN'T A SECRET. HARRISON AND VICTORIA DID NOT LIKE ONE another. If it were a competition for Harlan's attention, Victoria would win every time. She didn't mind exploiting it either.

While still in college, when Harrison worked for his father during summer breaks, she made a point to make her rounds to each employee. That is, everyone except Harrison. She wouldn't even glance at his office door. To everyone else, she was kind, although she was a bit awkward when it came to conversation.

The final snub for both was the used candle gifted to Harrison at Christmas five months ago. It was one of many reasons Harrison was surprised to see her name pop up on his cell phone this evening.

"How are you doing?" she asked after Harrison's greeting.

"All's well," he answered hoping she would get to the point if he didn't go into detail.

He thought, *What in the hell could she possibly need from me?*

Victoria, who was terrible at face-to-face conversations, was even worse on the phone. She shifted immediately into her reason for the call.

"Would you be willing to officiate a basketball scrimmage? This game is a reward for my students for maintaining good behavior this spring quarter."

Victoria was a teacher for the Indianapolis Public Schools and responsible for the severely behavioral handicapped students in the district.

Harrison understood her reasoning for the reward even if it wasn't truly honest. In other words, if none of them threatened to kill her, as happened often, she would agree to the game before summer break.

Victoria was good at her job and earned a specialist degree, just shy of a doctorate. Her responsibility was to teach them life lessons and coping skills to manage throughout a given day. If these kids could eventually blend into society, get a job keeping them off government subsidies, and out of jail, it would be a win. Victoria's classroom was their last chance before heading to juvenile detention. Fighting was what they knew best.

Realizing she was only using him, Harrison went along with the idea because he loved the game, and officiating high school basketball was a big part of his life. Just as importantly, she played to Harrison's ego. Yes, he could make this work even though Victoria was a bitch.

"Where are these kids from?" Harrison asked to get clarity.

"They're mostly from the inner city. Most come from broken homes. Many never had a father around to help influence their lives for the best."

I get it, Harrison thought condescendingly.

Victoria continued, "All of them had criminal records by the time they were fourteen."

Harrison laughed, "Do I need a whistle around my neck or a can of mace?"

Harrison had a lot of experience officiating basketball games. He was a well-established official in Indiana and licensed to work at the varsity level. He started when he was 18 and loved doing it to stay close to the game. Staying fit and earning some extra money also helped. He had extensive experience working many high-profile games, so the pressure wasn't an issue. Trying to keep from getting killed by these hoodlums, however, would be a new challenge.

"Ok, I'll do it," he told Victoria.

Victoria was pleased to hear him agree, although Harrison didn't recognize her appreciation.

Later that week, he drove to the Indianapolis inner-city YMCA on a Friday afternoon. The facility was barricaded behind a ten-foot tall, chain-link fence and appeared more like a high-security prison than a place for fun. Homeless drunks and garbage littered the street.

"I took a half-day off work for this?" he said out loud.

The scrimmage would run using high school rules, except no one would foul out. Upon arrival, Harrison realized quickly he was the only official asked to work the game when all games have typically three officials. When he asked Victoria about having only one official, she was surprised basketball games had more than one.

Harrison gave a nervous laugh. It's one thing to work a game alone if these were little kids, but these were nearly grown men with troubled backgrounds.

"Ok, but I'm not breaking up any fights," Harrison said to Victoria in jest.

"That won't be necessary. That's why I invited the police," Victoria stated as she pointed toward the nearest exit.

Harrison questioned his decision to officiate. Today was going to be something he would always remember – if he survived the day.

The game began, and the kids were having fun. It was a little rough at times, but Harrison called fouls and often explained the reasoning to the players. For the most part, the boys appreciated it and thought it was cool that a real official was working the game.

It went smooth except for one obnoxious player from Victoria's class. He disagreed with every call. The young man thought he was fouled on every missed shot and tried to instigate a controversy with Harrison or the opposing team. Although Victoria's team was coached by another teacher, he didn't try to calm the young man's tension.

"Man, I'd like to take you on right now," the kid shouted at Harrison during a break in the game.

"You mean, one-on-one?" Harrison responded.

"Damn right, one-on-one. I'll beat your ass, and you'll understand the definition of a foul after I get through with you," the youth declared.

The young man appeared more irritated with life than with Harrison, but this was the kid's opportunity to take it out on someone. Harrison knew a strong reaction could mean trouble, so he chose his words carefully and remained poised.

"I'll tell you what," said Harrison calmly. "You keep your damn mouth shut for the entire second half, and I'll grant you the request."

"So much for choosing my words carefully," he mocked himself silently.

Harrison didn't have to mention the issue to Victoria, who approached him at halftime to say he handled it well. He knew everyone was watching, which was another reason he tried not to humiliate the kid during the confrontation.

"Thank you for keeping calm," she told him. "I don't mind if you play him, but I'll need you to let him win. He lashes out because he lacks confidence, and then he can't control his anger during conflicts. He will fight as a result, and I don't want that to happen. Maybe he'll beat you anyway."

"Not likely." Harrison had already sized up the kid's game and was slightly offended by Victoria's statement.

The second half resumed and went much smoother than the first without the youngster saying anything. Instead, when he disagreed with a call, he glared at Harrison to get his point across.

This punk is asking for it, Harrison thought. *Screw it. I'm not letting him win. Victoria will be lucky if I let this kid hang close.*

He knew Victoria would seethe and knew she would run home and tell his father if he didn't follow her orders. Harrison didn't care. He was too old to be grounded. His ego got the best of him, and Victoria would have to get over it. It was time to teach this boy a lesson.

As soon as the game was over, the 17-year-old kid quickly approached Harrison.

"Game on," he stated. "You promised I could play you if I kept quiet. So, let's roll. I'm bustin' your ass."

Harrison looked at Victoria. She gave him a nod as a reminder of their conversation to let the boy win. Harrison politely nodded back.

"So I did," he replied generously to the young man.

The boy gave Harrison the ball first, and before the youngster knew what hit him, Harrison beat him 12-0. Game over.

Harrison noticed Victoria from the sideline glaring in disgust.

Harrison was grateful the police officer was watching when he sank the final basket. The boy lost his temper. Before Harrison knew it, the boy was coming after him. The officer stepped in just in time to secure the young man before he was able to land a punch.

Harrison never acknowledged Victoria as he collected his belongings and walked off the court. He smiled slightly, enjoying the fact he just crushed this young kid and put him in his place. Even more, he enjoyed putting Victoria in her place.

Victoria lost all respect for Harrison after that moment, but it was ok. The feeling was mutual.

SIX

"Toward the scorners He is scornful,
but to the humble he gives favor."

HARRISON AND CLAIRE WAITED ANOTHER MONTH TO REVEAL THE
baby news. The Marks were methodical people, and they wanted to make
sure they were safe from possible early complications before they shared
the news.

They were tempted to learn the gender, but they continued to fight off
their urge to pre-plan. The couple remembered what a distant family member once shared: "How often do you get to be as surprised as when you dis-
cover the sex of your baby when it arrives into the world?" – better words
were never spoken.

"We'll name a boy Adam," said Harrison during an afternoon walk in the
neighborhood. "If it's a girl, we'll name her Rebecca, or Becca for short."

"We'll talk about it," Claire added. It was fun to hear what Harrison suggested before she would have the final say.

"Who do you think it will look like?" Claire asked as if Harrison could
see into a crystal ball.

"It doesn't matter except for two things," Harrison stated. "As long as it's
healthy and loves basketball."

Claire tossed her head back and laughed at his wish list. The health aspect
was a concern, but she was convinced Harrison would be quite content with
a girl or boy who played the piano.

Harrison felt more content than he ever felt in his life. He was sharing
time with his perfect wife, who was carrying his perfect child. And, the

evening was perfect for a romantic stroll along their quiet lake. The wind splashed soft waves against the shoreline with a rhythm so soothing only God could be responsible. The sunset across the water only added to the breathless real-life art.

For the first time in a long time, Harrison was genuinely focused on God – something he didn't do very often.

This moment, however, could not be overlooked. "What if he or she wants to play soccer instead?" Claire inquired, knowing Harrison's dislike for the sport.

"Then I'll know the child was switched at birth," he shot back with more than a hint of sarcasm.

"How are we going to tell our parents?" Claire asked.

"It's entirely up to you how you tell yours, but I think we'll have dinner with my mom and Fred. I prefer to tell my dad and Victoria next month. You know there will be a mandatory birthday dinner coming up and Mimi will be there as well."

Harrison was kidding about the required birthday meal, but it was a fact, the family only came together for special events. Besides, Claire had an upcoming birthday.

"What about you?" he asked.

"Let's plan on going to Madison this weekend. I'm ready to share the news."

Claire was quite good at keeping secrets, but she was close to her mother, and she knew she would mistakenly spill the truth during an evening phone call if she didn't address it soon.

The trip to Madison went as planned. The small Indiana town nestled on the Ohio River seemed to welcome them as it never did before. The people of Madison were always kind but especially on this weekend, according to the Marks.

In fact, nothing changed at all except for Harrison and Claire's perspective. It was their moment to celebrate.

Most of all, this visit to Trinity United Methodist took on a different perspective as they sat through the morning service. The sermon hit home with them. Pastor Bob was so good at using personal stories for his congregation.

Harrison and Claire didn't have a church of their own in Indianapolis. It had a lot to do with excuses more than legitimate reasons. However, Madison offered a family environment that the Marks didn't feel was possible in the larger city. Church service in Madison was a way to fellowship, just as it should be.

Claire's parents were thrilled to hear the news of their eldest daughter and second favorite son-in-law as hugs were given and smiles were exchanged. Harrison even forced Claire's father into a hug, although he was not an emotional person by nature.

They shared the news with Harrison's mom and step-dad the following week to the same adulation.

Joanne always wanted grandkids and lots of them. They had one grand-daughter already from Harrison's step-sister. Now his mom wanted Harrison and Claire to get started. Three years of marriage was long enough to be on their own. If these country club grandparents were to spoil their brood of little ones, it all needed to happen while she was young. Harrison thought their persistence was humorous in the beginning, but then the topic became dreadful resulting in shorter phone conversations.

Doctor's appointments over the next month went smoothly for Claire. Morning sickness was almost non-existent, and according to Harrison, she looked radiant every day.

Comically, Harrison attended the first ultrasound appointment with Claire. They knew not to expect images of anything more than an inkblot. The couple wanted to hear the heartbeat together for the first time.

While sitting in the lobby, Emily Cross walked in and sat down for an apparent annual exam. Emily was a Communication student-teacher along with Harrison and Claire only a few years earlier at Butler University. Emily, a Phyllis Diller look-a-like, pretended not to know the couple and probably for a good reason. She married a doctor directly out of college and often bragged about how her "life was about to change." Harrison and Claire attended the over-the-top wedding highlighted by the release of doves.

It was the reception at the Downtown Marriott that caused a problem. Emily promised Harrison he could dance with the beautiful bride. She upheld her promise – much to the dislike of her jealous husband. The innocent laughs two friends shared proved to be too much for the groom. The doctor pushed himself through a crowd of drunken guests and toward the dance floor. He stood opposed staring at his bride and the villain holding his wife during a slow dance.

Rumor has it the two never consummated the marriage that evening since they spent the night fighting until dawn. Once they were willing to make-up, it was time to head to the airport and catch their flight to Aruba.

A full month passed, and sure enough, Harrison's father called his son to set up a birthday dinner for Claire at Mikado's, a downtown sushi restaurant. Harlan and Victoria were introduced to this Indianapolis staple by the state Senator, representing Indiana's 7th congressional district.

Harrison thought for a moment before he responded. "Are you sure Mimi will like sushi?"

"Oh, she'll love sushi," was Harlan's unexpected reply.

He should have made the argument to his father that seafood wasn't going to work for Claire. Her pregnancy eliminated foods from her diet she once liked. Now in the second trimester, she only craved foods that required ketchup. The young couple even ran through a fast food burger joint before dinner to satisfy her bizarre craving.

As Harrison and Claire parked the car for her 25th birthday celebration, he noticed that she had a troubled look on her face.

"What's wrong? Everything ok?" Harrison asked.

"I wonder what they'll do to embarrass us tonight?" Claire fretted.

"Don't worry about it," Harrison responded.

Deep down he shared the same concern. Everywhere they went with them something came up that would dissatisfy him or Victoria. At least the drama always gave Harrison and his grandmother something to talk about on their phone conversations for weeks to come.

After sharing greetings inside the restaurant, it only took 45 minutes for the older Marks to embarrass them. After giving their name, the Marks waited too long to be seated. Victoria didn't appreciate the delay. Waiting in line behind others was apparently beneath her and she requested the person in charge. The unsuspecting manager approached Victoria and Harlan.

Before Harlan could say a word, Victoria declared to the small-framed man for all to hear, "Do you know who I am? I am Victoria Marks, and I am the owner of Marks Medical Supply and multiple real estate properties in the Indianapolis area. My money and my name are well respected in this city, and I don't like having to wait this long for my table."

The manager's stunned look said it all to everyone in the lobby. The Japanese man tried his best to comprehend her comments. The frail manager scanned the room noticing all eyes were on him and awaiting his response to the overbearing woman.

In the meantime, Harlan stood defiant as his wife spoke on his behalf. He took a few steps forward and strategically aligned himself behind Victoria's shoulder. Harlan puffed his chest to show his support for his wife who had every right, even a responsibility, to speak her mind.

Hold your ground, Buddy, Harrison thought silently supporting the unsuspecting manager.

He did not hold his ground. As if his broken English weren't already bad enough, he was intimidated by Victoria and could barely speak.

He pulled the hostess aside, and they whispered something in their native tongue.

"He is not going to do this, is he?" Harrison said softly into Claire's ear.

"Yep." He answered his question as the manager personally motioned to the Marks to follow. The manager would even seat them himself.

Harrison felt the intense heat of onlookers as his shock turned to horror. His first inclination was to grab his wife and return to the car. He would have done it, but his grandmother was stuck. He wasn't going to leave her.

Like three people standing publicly in their underwear, Mimi, Claire, and Harrison walked to their table with their heads down and humiliated. Neither wanted to be associated with what just happened or the people that caused it.

"Head down and no eye contact with anyone," Harrison said to Claire to lighten the mood as they walked briskly to the table.

That wasn't going to happen. Claire was held hostage on her birthday to food she couldn't eat and people she didn't care to be around. The news of a baby took a backseat. If it were up to her, she would send them a birth notice upon the child's arrival and call it a day.

The tension was high as the entire Marks family sat down. Harrison noticed the manager giving instructions to the waiter assigned to the table.

"I bet he's telling him to spit in our drinks", Harrison mumbled to Claire.

Only small talk took place among the family even after dinner was served.

Near the end of the evening, Harrison finally mentioned to the unsuspecting three, "Hey, by the way, Claire and I are having a baby."

He never looked up from buttering his bread. He thought about sharing the news another day but that meant scheduling another appointment to spend unwanted time.

After the announcement, Claire scanned the table to gauge the mood. It was only Mimi who showed true joy. Harlan tried to show his happiness, but his excitement was overshadowed by Victoria's pathetic smile. Since the news had nothing to do with her, it didn't matter.

Harrison looked at his empty glass and half-empty wine bottle strategically placed nearby. On a normal evening he wouldn't have more than one drink, but this wasn't a normal evening. Harrison smiled to himself... If Claire was eating for two and couldn't drink the wine, then he had to pick up the slack.

SEVEN

"As water reflects a face, so a man's heart reflects the man."

THE SUMMER MONTHS WERE MIXED WITH JOY AND ANXIETY AS Harrison and Claire began prepping for a baby they lovingly referred to as *Thing One.*

Claire was growing bigger with each passing week and used a body pillow at night to sleep. While she looked great and her thin frame masked any swelling in the hands and ankles, there was no hiding that she was exhausted after waking up early and working all day. She had a desk job, but as a human resource manager, she was often on the plant floor speaking with employees. Comfortable shoes and elastic pants now replaced high heels and pencil skirts.

During the evening hours, Harrison attempted to connect with the unborn child by placing his head on Claire's stomach. Harrison loved music and loved to sing. He claimed to have a great voice, although Claire didn't concur. Nevertheless, it didn't stop him from singing his favorite songs that echoed through Claire's belly and into the ears of his captive audience. The baby began to kick and push during these less than magical moments. Harrison claimed it was out of pure joy for a song well sung. Claire was quick to mention he just disturbed a sleeping baby that was now active. Harrison would reluctantly play with the dog instead while she would try to relax. However, the restless child inside her stomach would continue to keep her awake.

Harrison stretched while trying to hold back a yawn. He fumbled for the remote and clumsily turned off the television. Swinging his arm toward the lamp on the nightstand, he hoped to find the switch without having to open his eyes.

Unaware of his surroundings, he didn't notice Claire sitting up and leaning against the headboard. She had been attempting to read a couple of articles on her iPad for the last 45 minutes, but Harrison's vocals were a distraction alternating between alto and bass. Now in the dark, her husband's insensitivity caused her to bristle. She forced him into a conversation.

"You're not even going to kiss me goodnight?" she questioned intentionally to disrupt his sleep.

"Lady, that's what got us into this predicament in the first place," he mocked referring to *Thing One* still churning in Claire's stomach.

Harrison hadn't fallen asleep and realized it wasn't going to happen anytime soon. His lovely bride was now poking him in the back to get his attention.

"You remember the block party tomorrow night, right?" she asked.

"Yes, of course," Harrison lied while slurring his words.

It was common for the residents of Hidden Shores to host holiday gatherings. The lake brought them together and created a common bond. All the neighbors especially took part on Labor Day weekend as it was the last celebration bringing an end to summer.

Harrison and Claire were the youngest couple in the small subdivision. The other couples who lived at Hidden Shores were Gen-X'-ers who had kids the same age as the Marks. They were empty nesters enjoying the final years of their career.

The people of Hidden Shores loved Harrison and Claire. In fact, they were intrigued by them. Many suspected a creative agreement was made to help them purchase their home, but they didn't care. The Marks were kind people who endeared themselves to the older generation. The community adopted the younger couple as their own.

Like many, Harrison and Claire voyaged in their pontoon boat the following evening to Joni Dobson's home. Her house was hardly modest as it stood two stories and expanded nearly the entire length of the property line. She recently completed construction on the home and she was eager to host the celebration if only to show it off.

The second-story deck looked over the spacious swimming pool below, making the house look even larger from the back. A three-car garage added girth to the already oversized home for a single lady with no children and three divorces.

"I'm doing it all wrong," Claire said with a sigh and looked as their boat drew closer to the shore.

Harrison knew what she was referring to and laughed at his chiding wife. Ironically, both knew it wasn't the multiple divorces that built the enormous showplace.

Joni knew people. Three years earlier, she was a realtor in Indianapolis and an average one at best. Joni struggled with clients who had a difficult time connecting with her personality. She was a brash woman that offended many people, although she never understood why. Joni was also beautiful, which often intimidated others, mostly women.

The stylish 52-year-old woman always pictured herself listing the high-end properties with the well-to-do in Indianapolis, but that never materialized. She bounced around from agency to agency after being fired for lack of production. Married women felt threatened by her beauty and condemned her flirtatious vibe. Married men tended to like Joni too much, which helped lead to all three divorces.

The saying in the real estate circle, however, is, "It only takes one client." If a realtor was able to land the whale, then nothing else mattered.

Harrison remembered a few stories about Joni. One particular evening, Joni entered the fitness center at her usual time. She drove home with an unsuspecting new member the evening before, and she was tired. Joni attended an exercise class hoping to work up a sweat outside the bedroom. That's where she met Victoria Marks.

The timing was perfect. Harlan was ready to take more vacations, and Victoria wanted him to back away from long work hours. The real estate market allowed that freedom. Harlan could handle business on the phone from his living room or, better yet, from a beach in Antigua. Attorneys and real estate agents could handle the paperwork. Harlan would be able to place them all in his back pocket once he established this new empire.

That's where Joni offered an advantage. It didn't take long for Victoria to introduce her to Harlan and he took the bait. Joni helped the Marks find their waterfront home at Hidden Shores. Their weekends were filled with dinners at each other's house and day trips to multiple Indianapolis suburbs to scout more potential real estate. They shared the love of sailing. So Victoria and Harlan welcomed Joni on extended getaways on their 34-foot Hunter sailboat docked at the prestigious Lake Michigan Yacht Club located 160 miles north.

One year later, the elder Marks executed their business venture. First, they purchased The Windsetter with 250 units. Four months later, they purchased Fox Trail with 150 units. The Huntsman Club, River Ridge, Wellman Arms, Meadowbrook Apartments, and Timber Falls completed Victoria and Harlan's stockpile within one year with Joni's help, of course.

When it was over, the Marks portfolio held $36 million in real estate assets. The down payments were courtesy of the medical business and area bankers were happy to lend the additional money for a handsome profit.

Joni was kind enough to drop her fees for her new friends, given their ability to purchase vast amounts of real estate in the Indianapolis market. In that time, Joni raked in better than $1.4 million from the transactions, minus some fees to her agency. She quickly rose to the top in her company and central Indianapolis.

The house the younger Marks were attending tonight wasn't the house the ex-husbands built. It was the house that Harlan built.

As one could imagine, Joni's favorite people in the small lake community were now Harrison and Claire. It was in her best interest, and she was going to make sure the pair knew it. While the other neighbors appreciated the younger couple for their friendship, Joni appreciated them for their relationship to her bottom line.

This came as no surprise to Harrison and Claire. They understood why Joni was so receptive, but it didn't matter because they liked her. She was quirky in a lovable and innocent respect, although there was nothing innocent about her. Her kindness to Harrison and Claire was a bit excessive, but that just added to her eccentricity.

Joni had no idea of the frustration Harrison felt for his father. As far as she was concerned, the Marks were a tight-knit family and Harrison was the heir to the fortune.

"We'll tell our neighbors tonight, right?" Claire joked as she used her finger to draw circles around her growing belly.

There wasn't going to be much to tell. People were going to notice regardless if the Marks wanted to share the news or not.

It was only one month ago Claire began to show. Pregnancy looked good on her. Friends and co-workers often declared their jealousy for this woman who was fortunate enough to have a body that hid the evolution of an unborn baby.

They hardly stepped off the pontoon when an entire crowd emerged and made them the focal point. The Marks felt like they were on display. Each person wanted to rub her tummy as if it would bring them good luck – just another reason for the people of Hidden Shores to open another case of wine and kill a few more beers. This was fine with Harrison, who favored the spotlight more than his wife. However, in this setting, he felt like the penguin exhibit at the zoo.

"We're all going to be grandparents!," one shouted, proving that Harrison and Claire were their own.

For the next hour, Harrison and Claire repeated the baby conversation again and again.

"Is it a boy or a girl?" each inquired.

"We don't plan on finding out until the birth," the Marks responded multiple times.

"Oh, you know the gender. You just won't tell us," most of the guests insisted.

The couple scanned the beautiful backyard looking for Joni, who was nowhere in sight. Harrison and Claire hadn't seen her in months, but she was aware her best friends were soon-to-be grandparents. Victoria and Harlan saw Joni often at the gym, dinner, or pursuing the latest real estate purchase. The young couple knew Joni would want to discuss the happy news.

"She's inside showing off the house," said one of the neighbors after Claire asked of her whereabouts.

It was true. Each person wanted individual tours, and Joni was happy to meet their request. She showed houses for a living. She certainly wanted to show her own.

"Maybe she already has an offer," Harrison stated, which caused a crowd of people to laugh aloud. Dumb dad jokes were a big hit with this crowd.

The Marks made their way toward the house. The graded slope from the lake to the house proved to be a formidable opponent for Claire, who was short of breath. She paused for a moment and turned around.

"What does the lake look like from this side?" she said softly pretending to care but silently regaining her wind.

Although she tried to cleverly execute the steep climb, she should have admitted defeat. Harrison pretended not to notice – no sense in upsetting the pregnant woman with whom he shared a bed.

"From this side we're not looking into the evening sun. It's pretty to see the light sparkle across the water," he added.

The pause allowed Claire the momentum she needed to get up the hill. Harrison smiled and said, "You made it!"

She furled her eyebrows and tossed a right elbow into her husband's side. He chuckled, knowing he deserved it.

The back patio was open, and they stepped inside. Walking directly into the open dining area overlooking the Tuscan style kitchen, the Marks took a seat at the bar and admired the view.

"Looks like your dad has helped improve her financial status," Claire whispered.

It was then Joni confidently whisked into the room and noticed the Marks sitting in her kitchen. As she began to offer greetings, Claire stood up.

Immediately, Joni was struck by Claire's appearance and changed her stride to slow motion. The smile on her face disappeared and changed to a look of surprise as she couldn't take her eyes off Claire's protruding stomach. Claire looked down, following Joni's gaze. She looked back up and realized the surprise in Joni's eyes.

Harrison stood back watched it all unfold. The one person who spends the most time with Victoria and his father had not been told of the good news. Joni was finding out about the pregnancy for the first time.

Too stunned to think clearly, Joni stated out loud, "I can't believe your parents didn't tell me you were expecting. They're going to be grandparents for Christ's sake!"

She recoiled and took inventory of Harrison and Claire's reaction. It was too late. Joni saw their shock turn to disappointment as the Marks realized their biggest news wasn't newsworthy to his father.

What kind of a father doesn't tell his friends he's about to become a grandfather for the first time? For every other family member, this is the biggest event of the year. What the hell? Harrison thought.

His thoughts were evident to Joni and Claire. Claire felt a deep sadness as well, but not for herself. She knew her husband's struggle as it related to his father. She felt the incredible disappointment Harrison endured as he tried desperately to compose himself. An awkward silence filled the room.

Just as Joni was about to speak and ask the same questions that had been asked by others, she was interrupted by another couple wanting anxiously to see the house.

"We'll talk more about this later," she now managed with a smile. "I am going to kill them for not telling me."

Conveniently for everyone, Joni and the other couple disappeared into the hall, and Harrison fell limp onto the barstool. He hung his head low, realizing the full extent of what happened.

"He hasn't told anyone, Claire," he said, disheartened. "He had nearly three months to brag about becoming a grandfather. If they didn't tell their best friend, then who have they told?"

"Let's get out of here," Claire interrupted. She grabbed his hand and whispered, "I don't want to be here anymore."

The two took full advantage of the dark sky to slip through the back yard. They weaved their way unnoticed past drunken neighbors and onto the pontoon. To avoid any unwanted attention, Harrison kept the lights off as the moon provided an ominous path directly home.

Claire had never seen her husband so dejected. He was the one who pulled her out of the doldrums. It was Harrison who had such a positive outlook on life and convinced her the bright side was always near. He attacked life in a way she didn't think was possible. That is what attracted her to him. It was hard, if not impossible, to rattle his inner strength. He was her rock. Now for the first time in their short marriage, their roles were reversed. He was heartbroken during a time that was supposed to be joyous. It was worse for Claire, as she didn't have an answer.

The best she could do was sit down next to her boat captain and put her arm around him. She didn't say a word; she didn't need to say a word. Harrison appreciated her effort and knew she had no solution. As Claire leaned her head against his chest, she felt a drop of rain fall on her cheek. She looked up and saw the stars shining brightly. There wasn't a rain cloud in the sky. She was feeling the tears drop from his face.

Without looking up and without saying a word, Claire gently reached over and grabbed Harrison's hand. She pulled it toward her and placed it directly on her belly. The baby kicked and tumbled causing them both to laugh ever so softly.

Claire had somehow known exactly what to do. She gave a subtle reminder to her husband that good things were on the horizon. She offered love and comfort, just when he needed it the most.

Harrison's tears continued to stream. Yet, what were once tears of great sadness now turned to tears of overwhelming joy.

"Thank you," he softly exhaled.

Claire, who was hugging Harrison, now clung to him tightly. It was an overwhelming moment of connection and profound peace. Stillness replaced anxiety. A deep sense of peace, wisdom, and understanding came alive and were no longer suppressed. Harrison felt protected and empowered to protect those he loved. His mind envisioned a path with clear direction. Harrison wasn't certain, but he felt another presence of something other than Claire. Divine love seemed to intervene and quiet his soul. Harrison believed he just felt the Holy Spirit for the first time in his life.

It would prove to be a significant moment and a much-needed introduction, as Harrison and Claire were about to face a test that would require God, Himself, to see them through.

EIGHT

"If a man digs a pit, he will fall into it:
if a man rolls a stone, it will roll back on him."

SUNDAY AFTERNOON WAS A DAY OF REST FOR VICTORIA AND HARLAN. Not for religious reasons, but more out of necessity. Catching up on chores, miscellaneous shopping, and visiting Harlan's mom needed to be checked off the list to start the week. If they were lucky, they could make time for a home-cooked meal to reconnect their relationship. It was a normal day given their busy work schedule and social agenda.

They planned to visit Harlan's mom after eating brunch at Patachou. But first, more running needed to be accomplished, and the Indianapolis Canal Walk was a bucket list before the end of the day. A visit to their wine store, purchased one year ago, wasn't necessary, but an errand they loved to do together so they could choose a bottle of wine for their Sunday dinner. On the way back, they always traveled through one of their many apartment complexes to ensure maintenance kept good curb appeal.

In reality, they were delaying the visit to see his mother. It was just something Victoria didn't prefer.

Harlan didn't call ahead. To do so would send her on a cleaning frenzy. Martha was a tidy person who always had her apartment looking like a showcase. There was no need for her to change the daily bathroom towels with guest towels. An unannounced visit would be fine.

Not long into the visit Harlan and Victoria both glanced at their matching Breitling watches when Martha wasn't paying attention. Martha didn't care if they were listening or not, she just wanted to see her son, that's all that mattered to her.

Daylight continued to burn as they sat visiting his mother in her modest two-bedroom apartment. He was her only child, and he knew what each visit meant to her. Martha carried on about her week without pause. The conversation was not a conversation at all but more of a one-way speech while Harlan and Victoria pretended to be engaged. After an hour Victoria made it painfully obvious to her husband it was time to leave.

"Honey, we have a lot to do tonight, and we have a busy day tomorrow. Also, Wolfie needs to go outside," Victoria stated matter of factly and partially blaming the couple's dog.

On the ride home, Victoria asked, "What's for dinner?" It was 5 p.m., and they still had plenty of time to enjoy their Sunday routine before diving into their hectic evening.

"How about stir fry?" Harlan mentioned. It was a quick meal, as long as both were willing to cut, chop, and cook.

"We have some of the ingredients at home, but we need vegetables," Victoria stated. "Drop me off at home, and I'll start chopping while you run to the store."

"Fine," said Harlan as he pulled into the driveway.

He was a bit frustrated and annoyed since they had passed two grocery stores on the way home.

He pulled the Jaguar close to the side of the house and opened the garage door.

Victoria made a point to let the dog out as priority number one. In her mind, she justified that she wasn't lying to Harlan's mother if Wolfie could be pushed out the door for a few minutes, even if he just stood on the patio.

She gathered the kitchen tools to pull the meal together and get a jump start before Harlan returned. Victoria soon realized the purpose of the

Sunday night meal had been defeated since she sent her husband on his way. She chuckled to herself and continued with the meal preparation.

The standard size poodle began barking, and Victoria realized Wolfie was still outside. It was unusual for him to bark, and she wondered if he saw a deer sprint through the yard since it was the harvest season. Victoria made her way to the patio door.

She called for Wolfie. Silence replaced the barking, and the dog was nowhere in sight.

She heard rustling in the distant bushes, and she became nervous and jittery. Victoria closed the door realizing her nerves got the best of her. She whipped her head around as now she heard barking from the front. She took a deep breath knowing everything was fine.

"Just get the dog inside," she thought, and she scrambled toward the front door.

Victoria went to open the door, but as it opened, she let out a scream that pulsated through her entire body. She nearly crumpled in terror. Victoria rapidly moved away from the door. She covered her head and retreated to the corner. She fell and feverishly screamed an inalienable tone.

Men dressed in black entered the house from the front door with guns raised. The back door was kicked open by two more men. They began shouting orders. "COVER THE HOUSE. CHECK UPSTAIRS. SECURE THE DOORS. NOTHING GETS OVERLOOKED."

"FIND HIM," was the only shout Victoria heard over and over while trying to catch a breath. The voices were cruel and intense. They were angry and they knew what they were after.

She couldn't think. Victoria had no idea what was going on. She only knew she was in danger. Adrenalin kicked in, but it wasn't helping her focus, it created more fear.

"What's happening?" she cried.

While trying to get her bearings, two men jumped on her pinning her head to the marble floor. She felt tremendous pain as a palm pressed relentlessly against her skull and another hand clenched firmly around her jaw.

Lying flat on the ground, she felt a crushing blow to her back. She could no longer scream. Not because she wasn't trying, but because she couldn't breathe. Quickly her arms were pulled behind her back. It felt as if her shoulders were pulled out of their sockets. She closed her eyes tight. She had no time to think about the pain. Fear wouldn't allow it. Victoria was terrified. She heard a sudden click from behind, and the bones in her wrist felt extreme pressure. Everything hurt, and she felt like she was about to pass out.

The shouts throughout the house subsided to a loud but instructional tone. Someone grabbed her shoulder and forcefully flipped her over. For the first time, Victoria was able to see the intruders. The men were wearing shielded helmets. Across the bullet proof vest read *Criminal Investigation, Department of Treasury.*

"WHERE IS HE? WHERE IS HE?" repeated shouts from the special agent, who was now nose-to-nose with Victoria.

His fists clenched her tattered blouse. He was on top and straddled her as she wiggled from side to side. The agent stood up and pulled her to her feet. He shoved her hard against the wall. Her head snapped back. She didn't need to see the bloodstain on the plaster to know how hard she hit the wall. Victoria let out a primal scream. The man was unforgiving and continued aggressive tactics.

"GET THE RING," he shouted to another agent.

From behind, strong hands gripped Victoria's wrist, forcing her fingers open. With a mighty jerk, she felt her diamond ring come off and she screamed louder. She tried to clench her fingers, but the hands behind her were too powerful to overcome.

Victoria Marks was now in full meltdown. She screamed uncontrollably as agents continued to secure the house and check drawers, cushions, cabinets, and anything else that would open. Keeping the showcase house pristine was not a concern.

The tension increased, and the agents became more agitated. They remained on high alert. The big prize was still unclaimed.

"SEARCH AGAIN!" demanded the lead agent. "IT'S NOT POSSIBLE!"

More than 10 agents in full gear resumed the frantic search and ransacked every inch of the home. One agent tried to talk to Victoria, but it was no use. She was curled on the floor in a fetal position. She continued to scream and sob, and her words were unrecognizable.

During a moment of Victoria's silence, the agents came to an abrupt halt. Tires squealed on the road directly outside the house. One agent ran to the door to see a Jeep racing from the house.

"DAMN IT! IT'S HIM! IT'S MARKS! HE'S ON THE RUN!"

Harlan was returning home. He was gone for nearly thirty minutes, and he knew his wife was waiting. Harlan made a slow turn into the subdivision. As he weaved around the corner heading for home, he noticed what looked like a box truck parked along the side of the street. He knew a parked box truck was unusual for a Sunday, especially in the evening. It wasn't blocking his driveway entrance, so he didn't give it much thought.

Victoria was likely getting impatient. He slowed down and drew closer. Dusk made it difficult to see. He peered toward his house and was surprised to see his front door standing wide open. Harlan knew something wasn't right. He noticed cars parked in his driveway blocking the garage entrance.

Something triggered and spiked his blood pressure. He was on high alert. Adrenalin kicked in once he recognized the situation. They were here for him.

He paused, but only for a moment. His mind exploded into chaos. He couldn't think clearly, but he knew right away he wasn't staying. To go inside would be suicide.

Thinking only about himself, he threw the car in reverse causing the engine to release the tires. The squealing rubber was indisputable. He knew right away he created unwanted attention. Harlan sharply turned the wheel causing the vehicle to jump a curb and travel into the neighbor's lawn. The car slid across the manicured grass.

Harlan looked to his driveway and saw men looking back. He had been spotted. Through the rear-view mirror, he could see the men racing toward their trucks. The chase was on, and this was one chase Harlan Marks couldn't afford to lose.

"What have I done?" he panicked and screamed out loud.

But he knew what he had done, and now it caught up to him.

He raced along the one-lane road passing houses, and his neighbors peered out windows. They noticed a Jeep that looked just like Harlan Marks's Jeep racing through their private community faster than the 25 miles per hour speed limit.

Harlan didn't notice the neighbors and he knew he had only seconds to spare. At this moment, he focused only on escape and survival.

He sped toward the main road. The winding roads appeared more like a prison gate, keeping him from a quick escape. Harlan jerked the steering wheel into the grass to avoid another car turning into the subdivision. The car hit a shallow ditch, but the force of impact jolted the vehicle up to the main road.

Of all the precautions the agents took to apprehend him, they didn't think to secure the entrance. In their haste upon his initial arrival, they never noticed Harlan switch cars after dropping Victoria. The Jeep was a toy that Harlan drove for fun. Since Victoria only enjoyed riding in luxury, Harlan drove his Jeep whenever he was alone and felt the urge. The Jaguar stayed parked in the garage.

"Where do I go?" he repeated to himself. His heart was hammering through his chest. He couldn't focus but kept driving as the evening grew darker.

Harlan barely noticed the other cars on the main road. He had no idea who was following him. Harlan wasn't aware of how close they were as he continued to check his rear-view mirror. His mind told him they were right on his bumper, and they knew his exact location. He feared they knew where he was going even though he had no idea himself.

Suddenly, he looked at his cell phone in the passenger seat. They could use the GPS to trace his phone. In a panic, he pitched the phone out the window, and it hit another car traveling in the opposite direction.

He didn't want to be caught. He couldn't be caught. He was so close to what he and Victoria considered their final destiny, and he needed to buy time. He had to find a way to make it until tomorrow morning.

The plane was scheduled to leave Indianapolis International Airport at 6 a.m. He and Victoria were supposed to be on it. He just needed to get there!

But now, Harlan was without the one person he needed the most. Those were details he needed to work out but now wasn't the time. He told himself Victoria would be fine. They didn't want her. She would somehow be able to join him later.

Harlan raced through intersections paying little attention to the color of the lights. Traffic on a Sunday night in Indianapolis was light unless you were involved in a desperate attempt to escape capture from the authorities.

He continued to check his mirrors to see if anyone was chasing him. His head was on a swivel. Swallowing was difficult. After multiple checks, he told himself he was safe. Harlan slowed down to a reasonable pace hoping to blend in with surrounding travelers.

He needed time to think. Before long, he realized he was a block away from his office. He knew they would have surveillance ready to capture him.

Going there would be a bad idea. He remembered a building close by that was currently abandoned.

He pulled around the back of the building, turned off the lights and sat. He had no plan. He couldn't reach out to anyone as he was sure there was an all-points bulletin out for his arrest. Besides, his phone was smashed all over the road.

Harlan reached for the radio and had the presence to turn on WIND, Indianapolis' AM news station. The news of his escape hadn't hit the public airwaves yet. He knew the APB was coming soon.

He shut off the Jeep and tried to think. There was now a manhunt for Harlan Marks. For the first time since he was a kid, Harlan began to cry.

He realized he should have taken the deal months earlier when his attorney interrupted his special evening.

NINE

"The man of integrity walks securely,
but he who takes crooked paths will be found out."

HARLAN MARKS RECEIVED NO WARNING WHEN SPECIAL AGENT Andrew Spawn walked into Marks Medical Supply 18 months earlier. He worked for the Criminal Investigation Division of the Internal Revenue Service and currently investigated suspicious activity at Harlan's business.

Spawn didn't have to travel far from downtown to call upon Marks. He walked through the front door and showed his badge to the receptionist ignoring her greeting. Common courtesy wasn't his forte. He was a man who thought highly of himself, and he had the credentials to prove it.

"I need to speak to Mr. Harlan Marks right this moment," Spawn demanded without a smile.

Two additional men accompanied the agent. They didn't need an introduction. It was clear their only responsibility was to back up Spawn and offer an intimidating presence. Not that it was needed.

The young receptionist, fresh out of high school, knew enough to walk back to her boss' office rather than page him or, worse yet, tell the agent Mr. Marks was too busy.

Harlan made them wait in his typical fashion. He had an idea of what they wanted since he had been receiving letters from Medicare stating the incontinent kits that Marks Medical charged the government was not reimbursable through the program.

The letters questioned the legitimacy of Medicare billing coming from Marks Medical. As a result, the Criminal Division of the IRS asked the company to cease and desist until further investigation. The letters had been piling up for six months, but after making an initial phone call to Medicare, Harlan ignored them.

According to Harlan, the rules governing Medicare were confusing. He felt that even the people who wrote the laws and regulations didn't understand what was legal and what wasn't legal.

Harlan argued his products met the required definition of an incontinent kit according to the written medical code. In Harlan's mind, he was meeting the standard because Medicare continued to reimburse him. They wouldn't continue to pay if he were out of compliance, right?

He suggested his actions weren't illegal just because the government operated under a broken system. If they were upset because he was exploiting a loophole, then it was their responsibility to fix the laws that govern reimbursement. Until then, he planned to operate under the current guidelines.

Defiantly, Harlan walked to the lobby. He stopped once he made eye contact with Agent Spawn, and without saying a word, Harlan motioned him to follow. Harlan intentionally walked well ahead of the three men and stood at his office door to usher them inside. He walked around his enormous cherry desk and sat down. Without being asked to take a seat, the three men helped themselves.

"I'm a very busy man," Harlan stated firmly. "What can I do for you?"

Andrew Spawn introduced himself and spoke on behalf of the two remaining men. Harlan didn't catch their names and he didn't care.

"You know why we're here, Mr. Marks," Spawn stated confidently.

"Actually, I don't."

"Mr. Marks, you've received numerous letters and had several phone conversations for six months advising you to halt your billing to Medicare, but you continue to do so."

"Yes, and they continue to pay me," Harlan responded. "You know I'm offering a service to Medicare patients covered by the Medicare system. A system they wrote. Now you want to tell me what I'm doing is illegal after following the rules written by bureaucrats? You're flat wrong, and you know it. They're upset they have to pay me for these services, and now you threaten me."

"Mr. Marks, I have been reviewing this case for some time. I must tell you this dangerously crosses the line. Your billing codes and the products you are providing to Medicare customers do not meet the standard definition."

Andrew Spawn held up a plastic baggie. Inside was a tube of hand cream, gauze pads, a barrier ointment, and a pair of surgical rubber gloves. In the other hand, Spawn held up a paper-thin adult diaper.

Spawn raised his voice intentionally. "Sir, you have been overbilling Medicare for these products and pawning them off as an incontinent kit. I can go to a drug store and purchase these items for much less than you're charging Medicare. This kit doesn't meet the requirement defined by our billing codes and is clear falsification."

"Wait a minute," Harlan met the same decibel level as Spawn and didn't appreciate being harassed. "Medicare sets the price for these kits. Not me. If they don't like having to pay that amount of money, they need to change the price."

Agent Spawn was unfazed by Harlan's tactic. He continued and raised his voice louder.

"It doesn't meet the required standard. You are selling drug store items and passing them off as kits. This is fraudulent. You, Sir, are bilking Medicare, and that's a federal offense. You will stop selling these kits immediately, or you will suffer the consequences."

Harlan pretended the last comments didn't catch his attention, but it did. However, he wasn't about to let on. Harlan Marks never backed down from a fight, and he wasn't about to start now.

Agent Spawn added to Harlan Marks troubles. "And further, since we first advised you of the illegal billing six months ago, you have been purchasing substantial real estate with the money you are bilking from Medicare. I suppose you think you can hide all this money, Mr. Marks?"

It was true. Harlan Marks did feel the threat of the federal government, yet his arrogance forced him to press ahead. Once he began receiving the letters, it didn't take him long to realize the predicament. Harlan sought a real estate agent and an attorney to help him transition out of one business and into another. Harlan thought playing the shell game with the IRS would complicate their case, and he could argue he was exiting the medical business per their request. He took a gamble the IRS might leave him alone. Instead, they took exception to Marks using Medicare money to purchase large sums of property.

"You can take it up with my attorney," Harlan stood up and pointed to the door. "Now get the hell out of my office."

Andrew Spawn sat for a moment without moving. He glared at Harlan Marks as Harlan stared straight back. Neither man was about to take his eyes off the other.

"You'll be hearing from us very soon," Spawn promised as he stood and exited the office. The two other men followed robotically in a straight line.

Harlan stayed in his office. He sat back and contemplated his next steps. He knew he would need a criminal defense attorney. Harlan was adamant this was all a misunderstanding on their part. Nonetheless, he had to protect himself and his fortune.

He picked up the phone and called his business and real estate attorney, Benton Jeffers. Harlan quickly brought him up to speed. Jeffers wasn't a criminal attorney by any stretch, but he could recommend a name.

"You want Jay Hausmann. He's experienced and proven. He deals specifically with white-collar crimes," Jeffers assured.

"First of all, I don't think I've committed a crime."

"I understand. I didn't mean to imply. I'm just telling you, if you want a great defense, he's the best," Jeffers said smoothing things over.

Jeffers made a lot of money from Harlan Marks over the past few years, so he tried to be respectful but firm.

"But you need to understand, Harlan. Hausmann doesn't come cheap. You're looking at a $100,000 retainer fee and then $700 per hour."

"I'm not worried about the cost. I have the money. Thanks," Harlan hung up the phone without saying goodbye in his typical farewell.

Harlan would think about the situation for the next 24 hours. In an unusual fashion, he shared his day with Victoria once they settled in for the night. Victoria was alarmed. She was aware of the letters and knew about the phone calls. She was also heavily involved in the transition away from the medical business and into real estate and she fully understood the reason behind the decision. She had an obvious concern when this began but was able to brush it off. There was no hiding it now. Victoria realized this just went to another level. Harlan was still able to convince her the government was irritated with his success and used today's intervention as a scare tactic.

"Victoria, I assure you we've done nothing wrong," Harlan said firmly. "But we need to hire an attorney to help straighten this out. In the meantime, we are going to continue our plan to transition into the real estate market."

Victoria was a strong woman, but she was submissive when it came to her relationship with her husband. She loved his confidence and reassurance in every matter. She recognized his strength when it came to making a difficult decision. Harlan always took charge when she knew she couldn't do the same. Overall, she trusted him. Once Harlan explained the situation, Victoria agreed the responsibility was entirely on the Medicare system. His arrogance often rubbed off on her as she followed blindly.

Sleep didn't come easily for either that night. Each pretended to be asleep while contemplating the possible outcomes.

Victoria turned away from Harlan and anguished in silence. She couldn't help but think back to simpler times. She was a selfish woman. There was no question about that accusation. However, she was convinced things had gone too far. They crossed the line, and now her husband was going to pay. The only question in her mind was the total cost. *What was at stake? What would be the collateral damage?* She didn't have the answers and that scared her.

Harlan wouldn't allow himself to consider the worst-case scenario. To him, losing his wealth was too much to handle. He had worked too hard. Harlan became accustomed to the money, the houses, the vacations, and the toys that defined his lifestyle. In his mind, he was gaining respect and notoriety from people that mattered.

For a moment, Harlan considered praying in desperation. He considered dropping to his knees and asking for a fix. However, he quickly reconsidered knowing it would be a waste of time. Harlan needed immediate action, not false hope.

Besides, he had plenty of hope. What could a god do for him? He needed the best attorney.

"Hausmann will make this go away," he convinced himself.

Although sleep was out of the question, he was able to rest for the remainder of the night.

Harlan wasn't too far off with his evaluation. Jay Hausmann did have pull and a damn good reputation in the tri-state area. Hausmann was 56 years old and in the prime of his career. His name caused waves with prosecuting attorneys and commanded respect with high-ranking judges, a couple of whom Hausmann went to school at the University of Michigan Law School.

Harlan and Victoria contacted him the following day and asked for a meeting. When he heard the IRS was involved, he obliged immediately. White-collar criminal law was his passion and made up 100% of his portfolio. This was another opportunity to beat the government and pad his wallet along the way.

Two days later, they met in Hausmann's office in downtown Indianapolis near the courthouse. The Marks took comfort as they stood in the lobby and admired the offices' architecture. The décor represented the firm's success, which dates back to 1990 according to a plaque behind the receptionist.

Jay Hausmann confidently walked over and firmly shook hands with the couple. Hausmann carried himself with tremendous poise and assurance as his resume gave him good reason. Hausmann's 6'3" frame was accentuated by broad shoulders and a long torso.

Immediately, Harlan recognized that his suit was crafted with the finest Italian silk and tailored to his physique. Hausmann's salt and pepper hair added to his sophistication, while his steel blue eyes penetrated anyone who stood opposed.

After he extended his hand for greeting, he escorted Victoria and Harlan down the hallway to the conference room. His secretary brought coffee and other beverages.

Hausmann then turned around to Harlan and said, "Once this is over, we'll celebrate with a bottle of wine."

The Marks smiled. His was hope taking action. In Harlan's mind, Hausmann became the god he needed.

The convincing attorney agreed to take the case, provided the funds were transferred to his firm at Fisher, Comer, and Scarffe within the next 48 hours. Harlan and Victoria left the office knowing they would need to attend more meetings to bring the experienced lawyer up to speed. But they both felt Hausmann had this under control. They held hands as they walked out of the gigantic firm and smiled at one another. Both felt relief that everything was going to be just fine.

Jay Hausmann contacted Special Agent Spawn and advised him that all concerns would now be directed to him. If any contact was made directly with his client, it would be considered a breach of due process and be reported immediately. It was a short conversation as Hausmann intended it.

He knew Spawn had zero love for him. Hausmann used the phone call to do more than just warn his adversary of the news. He used the call to get a reaction.

Andrew Spawn didn't take kindly to receiving instructions, especially from a person he considered an enemy to the government. He traveled this path before with the powerful attorney when the IRS lost to Hausmann. Hausmann picked the government's case apart two years earlier in an insurance scam where the accused CEO of a major Indianapolis based company stood to go to prison for a minimum of 20 years. A sympathetic jury and a few restitution dollars later, the high-profile businessman was out of a job, but received a handsome severance package that paid for his sprawling retirement home in Hilton Head, South Carolina overlooking Calibogue Sound. Spawn was prepared to do battle this time with an aspiring U.S. Assistant Prosecuting Attorney, David Costello.

Costello was 35 years old and looking to make a name for himself. His red hair, pale white skin, and his knack for picking out cheap suits didn't do him any favors when it came to becoming an elite prosecutor, but he could hold his own in a court room.

He was aggressive and a quick study, according to his peers. This was the case that could catapult his career. He would be representing the IRS. Harlan Marks would be brought to justice.

It took almost two weeks for Hausmann to educate and arm himself before meeting with Costello and Spawn. As expected, Hausmann was fully prepared. He knew the IRS didn't have the manpower to go further with anything other than allegations against Harlan and Victoria Marks based upon the existing Medicare rules.

The U.S. Assistant Attorney knew it too once he took the time to review the case against Marks. An offer would have to be made on behalf of the government to cut the Marks a deal.

The idea of a deal didn't sit well with Agent Spawn, who felt he did too much work over the past few years to have it come to such an anti-climactic ending. Costello had a hard time convincing him after they met with Hausmann.

"You don't have a case against my client. Investigating Harlan Marks, and Marks Medical Supply, will take too many resources even if your allegations are true which, of course, they are not," Hausmann smiled upon this latest reveal.

He continued, "You're wasting money and time on my client, and you will go down in a ball of flames again if you decide to take this any further."

Hausmann never turned his eyes away from Spawn daring him to respond. Spawn didn't disappoint.

"You son-of-a-bitch!" Spawn verbalized ever so slowly but in a tone that could haunt.

The deal was already bad enough. But losing to Hausmann a second time was too much to stomach. Hausmann was the same man who had already beaten him and likely cost Spawn a promotion.

Costello jumped in before his client erupted. "Mr. Hausmann, you are correct that our resources within the criminal division of the IRS aren't what we desire. To tell you otherwise would be a lie," Costello declared. "We are aware you know better. However, please don't be mistaken. We have what we need to move forward with a case against Mr. Marks and his wife."

Everyone in the room stood silent.

"It has taken the better part of two years to investigate because Special Agent Spawn has been one of only a few working this case since it came to our attention. If we had more individuals working this case it wouldn't have provided us more information, but we would have brought this forward a lot sooner."

It was a convincing argument. Hausmann would have made the same argument if he were in Costello's position. Hausmann also knew, despite what Harlan Marks argued, his client was taking advantage of the system. The government agency had the money and determination to see this case to the end. Hausmann knew that prison time was highly plausible if this issue wasn't handled with complete transparency.

Hausmann, however, remained silent. Being a savvy attorney meant knowing what to say and when to say it. It also meant sometimes saying nothing at all and now was precisely one of those times. He knew a deal was coming.

"However, the government is willing to offer Mr. Marks a deal we feel is reasonable," Costello replied right on cue.

Costello waited for the attorney to respond, but Hausmann was content to sit and listen.

"Your client must cease and desist with his Medicare business immediately upon signature of the agreement."

Costello paused again to make sure the message was clear to Hausmann. He wanted to ensure the attorney understood before he went on to the most critical piece of the deal.

"Further, Mr. Marks must pay restitution of $8 million payable to the IRS within a three-month period from the time of the agreement. Should he say no to this agreement or fail to meet the requirements of this agreement, the government along with the IRS and myself, will be forced to pursue this as a criminal matter. All deals will be off the table," Costello said with emphasis on the last sentence.

"Now, do you understand?" he added while sliding the formal agreement across the conference room table.

Hausmann took a mental note of the action from the much younger attorney and looked away. He pretended to stare out the window from the 14th-floor window of Fisher, Comer & Scarffe.

The deal wasn't horrible, but he was hoping for a better offer. $8 million is a lot of change, but he was well versed in his client's bank account and overall self-worth. Marks would have to rely heavily on future real estate income. He also knew the deal would force Marks to sell most of his properties to create immediate cash to pay the penalty.

Harlan Marks had wealth but not the kind that was considered liquid. The deal would severely damage his client if it didn't bring him to the brink of bankruptcy. At least Hausmann could keep him from jail. Further, if Marks was the entrepreneur Hausmann believed him to be, there was always an option to pursue another career path.

Hausmann looked back to Costello. The prestigious attorney knew he was anxious for a response. The younger attorney tried to hide his nerves, but the more experienced Hausmann could see through him.

Additionally, an attorney doesn't become an elite defense attorney without having contacts on the inside. Jay Hausmann was well connected inside the IRS who respected him enough to share some of the agency's major concerns in the Marks' case.

The fact was the government was embarrassed by Harlan's exploitation of Medicare. They wanted to punish him, but they also needed this case to go away quietly. The IRS had to do whatever it could to make the case look like a victory. Not only for the general population, but it had to be a victory to the executives inside the government agencies who previously suffered humiliating public defeats.

Also, knowing the IRS didn't understand its own Medicare rules while allowing someone to bilk them for at least $15.5 million would bring further embarrassment to an already damaged government agency.

Hausmann began nodding his head slowly after he pondered the proposal.

"I don't think this deal is fair for my client, but I agree it's not altogether unfair. I will take this proposal forward," he said. "However, we both know there is room for further negotiation. I suspect we will be meeting again soon. However, this is a starting point."

Jay Hausmann stood to shake hands with both men. Costello professionally accepted his hand while looking him in the eyes. He gathered his stack of folders and saw himself out.

Andrew Spawn stood slowly and forced himself to shake hands with the decorated attorney. Hausmann enjoyed every moment of Spawn's struggle. The much taller Hausmann looked down upon the smaller man who refused to look up. Without saying a word, Spawn gave a firm shake and exited the room.

"I love my job so much. I can't believe I get paid," Hausmann quipped to irritate Spawn as he walked away.

"I can't believe they pay you either," Spawn replied quickly not to be outdone.

He remained straight-faced and continued to walk out of sight.

Hausmann let out a big laugh. He didn't know Spawn had it in him to think so quickly on his feet.

Hausmann would have to sell this initial proposal to his client right away. He would call him that evening to schedule an appointment for the next morning.

"So, we have a deal on the table," Hausmann announced once Harlan Marks answered the phone. "When can you and Victoria get together?"

The Marks were exiting the Marriott Hotel where Harlan was honored and delivered the keynote speech for the 12th Annual Indianapolis Business Association Banquet. He needed to know the results of the meeting.

"Tell me now." Harlan Marks said firmly. He was never a patient man, and this was no time to start.

"Can we just get together in the morning?" Hausmann questioned.

"Now."

Hausmann shared the details as best he could since he had to alter his approach.

"That's not what we discussed Jay," Harlan said convincingly. "I offered $4 million."

Victoria heard the conversation. Even though she didn't hear the details, she knew her husband's tone. She was surprised by Harlan's response as she thought any deal that kept her husband, and possibly herself, out of prison would be a good ending. Harlan walked further away to carry on the private conversation. Victoria could no longer hear what was said. After the initial exchange, it was fine with her.

"I'm not paying any more money, losing my medical business, and turning over the properties. They still have no idea what rules apply, and I'm not interested in bailing them out of their mess."

Hausmann couldn't believe what he was hearing from his client.

"Listen. I think we have room for negotiation, but you should realize that you will lose your business regardless of what happens. It's getting shut down. It's over," Hausmann declared. "It's the IRS and a special agent who would like to mount your head over his fireplace as a personal trophy. They are giving you a way out. If you don't take the deal, it could turn out better for you, but it could also turn out much worse."

Hausmann continued, "They don't have the manpower, but they do have all the necessary money to keep dragging this out. They may not win in court, but they sure as hell will try. Besides that, Harlan, they'll be more than happy to bankrupt your sorry ass in the process, and you'll realize you're more broke than losing a company, $8 million bucks, and a few properties."

"They're not going to take this forward. They don't want this to go to court any more than we do. You said yourself they don't have the resources. We are not taking the deal. You know my offer. Get it done," Harlan stated and ended the call.

Harlan didn't even shiver. The government could have Marks Medical Supply. He would find an alternate plan, but he would not let them touch his real estate company that ensured his financial freedom. Without the real estate, he would have nothing more than where he started years ago. He couldn't go back to that life. Not only would he decline the offer, but he would also continue to funnel Medicare money into additional real estate.

Regardless, he needed an alternate outcome, and it was Jay Hausmann's problem to fix.

TEN

"The violence of the wicked will drag them away,
for they refuse to do what is right."

Harlan Marks was now a man on the run. He couldn't shake the feeling that his escape was temporary. The night began to fall, and the temperature dropped as he considered his options. Feeling sorry for himself was not an option.

Uncertain and with fear settling in, he checked the locks on the door for the third time and rested his head against the steering wheel. He paused and told himself to relax. Time was critical. Every move over the next 12 hours would require steady nerves and a strategy. He had to disappear. He had to catch that plane tomorrow morning.

The money was secure in two places. The first was a bank in Mexico. The second was an offshore holding trust established in his next place of residence, the Cayman Islands.

Once Harlan and Victoria realized the government wasn't giving up on making an example out of them, they began immediate wire transfers of their nest egg. The Cayman Islands were considered a haven that protected personal assets from the United States Government.

However, he failed to recognize Andrew Spawn's visibility to his bank accounts, as funds continued to be pulled systematically in consistent sums of $5,000 and $10,000. As he gathered himself, Harlan realized fleeing the U.S. was becoming less of an option.

The longer he sat, the more he knew the authorities would find him. Harlan still had his billfold and his credit cards, but they were worthless. If he used them, he would be swarmed by agents at gunpoint within minutes. Fortunately, Harlan always kept a wad of cash in his billfold. He didn't use the cash. Harlan wanted waitresses and cashiers to see his cash as he opened his billfold and reached for the plastic. Now it would come in very useful as he considered his next move. Harlan had over $500 in $50 bills that would ensure his anonymity through the night.

His mind drifted as he worried about his safety and Victoria. He questioned his clarity when he threw the cell phone out the window. He could use it right now, but that would be a dead giveaway to his whereabouts.

Harlan glanced at his watch. He couldn't stop fidgeting. It was either nervous energy or maybe his drive for survival. On a normal night, he would be preparing for bed at this time.

He wasn't sure what else to do. Whatever it was, it kept his mind from hearing suspicious noises from outside the vehicle.

The pressure mounted with each passing minute. If the IRS investigators and the authorities found him, it would be over. He criticized himself for fleeing the house, which was now hours ago. If he stayed, maybe this would all be over. The misunderstanding would be sorted out and would prove that Harlan had nothing to hide. That possibility was in the past now that he was on the run.

It was a moment of panic that cost him severely. With the money transfers and mocking the U.S. government over the past two years, it likely didn't matter. He challenged them, and he pushed them too far. Harlan Marks had the Criminal Division of the IRS and the U.S. Assistant Attorney bristling because of his arrogance and defiance.

In frustration, Harlan exited the vehicle. He began walking toward downtown Plainfield located three miles away. Dressed in shorts, a t-shirt, and sandals, he prepared himself for the cold journey to find a hotel.

He knew he couldn't walk the road as somebody could get suspicious and report it to the nearest authorities. He walked off the road and along tree lines. His body quickly began to shiver as he projected the temperature to be well below 40 degrees on this autumn night.

Although he was safe, Harlan couldn't help but keep a lookout. He was concerned every passing car could see a shadow of a man along the side of the road. Imaginary footsteps were creeping up behind him, and he felt panic setting in once again.

Harlan stopped and pressed his head against a tree. He needed to remain focused.

Gathering his senses and grasping for clarity, he trotted toward the woods. It was a quicker path as long as he could negotiate fallen branches, mud holes, and anything else he might encounter.

While fear subsided, worry remained. Harlan stopped and closed his eyes to steady himself.

"Control your breathing," he told himself out loud.

He knew he was on heightened emotion, but the fact he was a 56-year-old man running through the woods was taking its toll. He gripped his billfold tightly to make sure he still had it and trudged ahead.

After navigating through miles of woods and two large cornfields later, Harlan saw the lights of Plainfield and a Red Roof Hotel sign. It appeared closer than it looked, but it was at least in sight.

He gasped for air once he arrived in the parking lot of the hotel, and sat down on a bench near a side door. He had to calm his breathing. He also needed to collect himself before entering the lobby and requesting a room.

Harlan looked at his watch one last time. It was 10:26 p.m. He had been on the run now for more than 4 ½ hours.

Where was Victoria? he wondered.

She had to be worried about him. Harlan let it go. He didn't think they would take her into custody. However, he couldn't be sure.

He continued to remind himself he was a hunted man. They wanted nothing to do with Victoria. They were using her to get to him. He was supposed to be in the house when they converged. Harlan was sure the agents moved on to pursue him while keeping surveillance on the property. Regardless, he was sure Victoria was safe.

Using his best sales approach, Harlan Marks entered the Red Roof Inn with a smile. He gave the night clerk no reason for concern when he made eye contact.

"One room, non-smoking, if you have it, please."

Harlan leaned in and placed his elbows upon the counter. The young lady in her mid-twenties went to work and found a room on the 2nd floor.

"Sir, that will be $72.00 plus tax bringing your total to $77.04," she smiled and asked the older man if it would be cash or charge.

"Cash," Harlan placed two $50 bills in front of her as she made change.

Once complete, he turned toward the hall. The pain and sadness quickly returned to his face.

The room door squeaked as it opened and then slammed shut behind him. It had the ominous sound of a cell door trapping him without re-entry into the free world.

Harlan sat on the bed, broken and exhausted. He opened and closed his eyes – with each blink he was hoping to see a different reality emerge. He made no other effort; he just wanted to feel safe. He closed his eyes one last time and fell back onto the bed. His breathing was finally under control and he laid still and stared at the ceiling.

"I don't know what to do," he whispered.

Any hope that he held onto began to fade with each pounding heartbeat. Harlan clenched his teeth to keep from screaming. He hated himself right now, but more than hating himself, he hated Andrew Spawn.

Spawn, along with David Costello, was the zealot who couldn't let this go. Harlan transitioned out of the medical business just as the special agent requested. At least that's what his mind told his heart. He didn't do anything wrong. The government was using him to prove a point. They wanted to make an example out of an innocent man, and he drew the short straw. They were the ones to blame.

He was tired, but he also knew sleep was out of the question. Men were actively searching for him. His thoughts bounced back and forth between his money and his wife. How much did Victoria tell them? Harlan was certain that she broke down and shared their plan. Spawn had to know they were planning to flee the country the following morning. The timing was too perfect. If he thought the morning flight was an option before, it was now out of the question. Agents would be ready for him at the airport security checkpoint.

Harlan considered different scenarios. He knew how bad things could get. His best option was to come up with the least bad option.

Before he knew it, his body was drenched in sweat. His flesh began to burn, and once again, he was gasping for breath. The guilt, the anger, and the confusion haunted him as he made his way into the bathroom.

He turned on the light and was stricken in horror to see the man staring directly back in the mirror. Harlan didn't recognize himself. He appeared defeated. The once confident man now stood with his shoulders slumped. The same man once surrounded by the wealthy and elite now faced himself without a friend in the world.

Harlan felt his knees weaken. He crumpled to the tile floor. Shaken by the experience, he became nauseous. Harlan reached for the toilet lid and thrust his head into the bowl. Grabbing a hand towel from the bottom shelf, he wiped his mouth, curled up on the floor in a fetal position and sobbed.

It finally hit him – he was not just a husband and a business owner. He was also the son of an elderly mother. His mother who may not survive after hearing the news of her only child. He was a father who was supposed to set an example for his son to whom he had given little attention over the years. He knew he couldn't fix this problem by throwing money at it. He could only do what he always did in the past. He would clear it from his mind.

At that moment, Harlan Marks made a decision. The best course of action was to turn himself over to the authorities the next morning.

Angry that he allowed himself to break under the pressure, he stood up and again looked in the mirror. He straightened his hair and threw water on his face. Harlan noticed the shower behind him. He stripped off his clothes and turned on the hot water. He plugged the drain and poured shampoo under the running water. Harlan prepared the last bath he would have in a very long time.

He fell asleep in the tub. For nearly two hours, Harlan had the best sleep that he had in months. If it had not been for the cooling water, he would have slept longer.

As he pulled himself from the tub and wrapped the over-sized towel around his frame, he walked into the room. Dawn was breaking through the window and shed light on the unused hotel bedroom. He crawled under the covers to warm up and thought about how the day would unfold. Harlan drifted off once again without knowing the time. He was at peace with his decision.

The clock on the nightstand read 9:16 a.m. when he awoke. The morning sun was in full swing as it peered between the drapes and into his eyes.

Harlan sat on the edge of the bed and dressed in the same clothes as the night before. He took advantage of the hotel's continental breakfast and stuffed himself with waffles, eggs, bacon, and juice.

With his billfold in hand, he walked next door to Target and purchased a new wardrobe to wear for the day's big event. He wanted to look good. Upon re-entering the hotel, he asked the clerk for a toothbrush, toothpaste, a razor, and shaving cream, and went back to his room.

Once he settled, he used the hotel phone to contact Jay Hausmann at the law firm of Fisher, Comer & Scarffe.

"Jay, this is Harlan Marks. You need to come and get me." Harlan provided the address for the Red Roof Inn.

The wait seemed like an eternity. Harlan knew this would be his last few moments of freedom. He sat on the edge of the bed and tried to think of a worse time in his life. He could only think of one.

ELEVEN

"Do not boast about tomorrow,
for you do not know what a day may bring forth."

MARTHA AND DUDLEY MARKS WERE NOT HIGH SCHOOL sweethearts, although they graduated from the same school at the same time in Warren, Ohio. Martha and Dudley weren't even friends.

Martha Randel wouldn't be caught with a nerd such as Dudley Marks. She had a social circle and a reputation to maintain. Even speaking to a boy such as Dudley would have instigated an immediate downgrade in social status.

During her senior year, Martha was the Homecoming Queen and runner-up at the Winter Snowball. She regained the top honor the following spring as Prom Queen from her arch-nemesis, which solidified her place in Warren G. Harding High School lore.

She attended Ohio University in Athens, Ohio in the fall of 1953 and began looking for her future husband. She had no intentions of declaring an official major. At the time, it was the respectable thing to do for a young lady who didn't plan on being a nurse or an elementary school teacher. If necessary, she was willing to take a secretarial job until she became pregnant with her future husband and began raising a family.

Without a doubt, Martha was going to school to find a man to take care of her and allow her the opportunity to stay home, raise a family, and most importantly, get her out of her small Ohio town.

Dudley Marks attended the same university starting the same year. He didn't want to attend college, but his mother and father wanted more for him.

If it were up to Dudley, he would begin working on the line at the local steel mill where his father worked as a mid-level manager. His father thought Dudley could begin as a supervisor and have more opportunities for advancement with a college degree. They had the money, and his parents thought Dudley could use the experience to grow socially before coming back to their blue-collar town.

Honestly, his parents were worried about him. He had little social skills. He could use the extra four years to mature as a man.

Dudley was a self-conscious man. He was already showing a receding hairline at 18 years old. By the time Dudley was 27, the poor man would be bald like his father and his father before him. He never did anything wrong in high school, and he didn't participate in extra-curricular activities. Dudley was an amazing athlete, according to his father, but he was too shy to play in front of a crowd. He couldn't sing and couldn't play an instrument, nor would he consider trying.

At one time, Dudley studied the possibility of joining the chess club until he found out Allison Ingram, who was often making eyes at him during government class, was also on the team.

College could provide the stage where Dudley Marks could break out of his shell and grow into a man. Secretly, his father was hoping all this and more.

"Go out at night and have a beer or two," his father said pulling him aside. He took out a pack of cigarettes and nestled them inside his son's shirt pocket.

"Smoke a few. It will help you fit in," he continued.

Dudley was horrified at the counsel his father was giving him, but the worst advice was about to come.

"Find a pretty girl. Hell, find a girl that's not so pretty. It'll give you a boost of confidence like you've never felt before." With a loving slap on the side of the face, his father turned away from Dudley leaving him in the hallway dorm to join his wife in the car.

Dudley's mom was sobbing uncontrollably at the thought of leaving her only child at college with no one to care for him. Her wadded up tissues were strewn about the front seat to prove her misery. Her husband knew she wasn't crying for the boy. She was crying for herself and the idea that she was now an empty nest parent.

While Dudley wasn't about to take his father's advice, he did have some fun. He joined an academic fraternity thinking it could help his already unparalleled study habits. It also introduced him to new people much like him. Seven guys would meet on the 5th floor of the library Monday through Thursday at 6 p.m.

They soon discovered that they enjoyed basketball and thought they should put together an intramural team for the upcoming winter. It wasn't Dudley's idea, but he reluctantly went along. It was a hit. Dudley didn't have to play in front of large crowds, and he would get to play with people who liked him.

He became an instant intramural star. Basketball was his favorite game, and he used to spend hours dribbling and shooting in the driveway. Dudley's team won every game against the other fraternities, and at the end of the season they reached the intramural championship game. Although he and his buddies fell to the athletes on the Ohio University football team, he enjoyed the competition.

During one of the games, a cheerleader for the Ohio University basketball team watched this 6'2" athletic man while her squad was practicing. During a break, the cute young woman stood courtside as this handsome man ran up and down the court against a team of fraternity hotshots.

Once the game was over, the young man walked off the court toward the nearby water cooler. Of course, Martha had to speak first.

"Don't you know when a girl is flirting with you?" she asked quizzically with a flirtatious grin.

"I'm sorry?"

"I was standing over there watching you play and wandered over here to get a drink of water at the same time as you. Doesn't that mean anything to you?"

"Uh, you like basketball, and now you're thirsty?"

Martha recognized his innocence immediately and knew he wasn't mocking her. She found it refreshing, but most importantly, she also found it attractive.

Most attractive boys came on too strong for her taste. All the nice guys were too short, too fat, too dumb, and certainly not strong enough to handle her personality. This one was different. He had a quiet confidence, yet his modest approach was very appealing.

"What's your name?" she asked while hoping the conversation would lead somewhere.

"Dudley Marks."

"Where are you from Dudley Marks?" Martha now asked as she leaned in and smiled.

"Warren, Ohio. How about you?" he managed to muster.

"Oh Lord," she gasped in disbelief as she placed her hands on her hips.

"I may not get out of that town after all," she added with a grin.

Martha and Dudley had their first date two nights later. They would never be separated again. Dudley convinced his best and only girl to stay in school, and they graduated together. The diploma came as a shock to Martha's parents, who knew her intentions from the day she left for school. They were pleased with Dudley's influence on her.

Likewise, Dudley's parents couldn't have been happier. Their awkward son didn't just find a pretty girl but also found a pretty hometown girl. It earned Dudley an elbow to the ribs from his father every time he brought Martha home for dinner.

They married in June 1957 after spring graduation. Dudley went to work as a supervisor at Republic Steel. They purchased a house in a desirable neighborhood giving Martha what she wanted. The next project was to start the family she always desired.

Dudley wanted to wait a year before thinking about having a child. He was a meticulous man and told Martha he had a five-year plan.

Dudley never shared the details of the plan as he never really had one. However, he knew he had to slow his wife down. He needed more time to adjust to the nuances of being a full-time working man and husband. Dudley held her off for 10 years before Martha finally insisted that they start a family.

In the meantime, Martha moved her now-widowed mother into the enormous two-story home on Washington Avenue. Dudley didn't have any say in the matter, but his easy-going demeanor made for a smooth transition.

They welcomed Harlan Howard Marks on February 16th, 1967. Dudley and Martha Marks were 32 years old.

Dudley and Martha always provided a loving home for their son. Harlan was adored as the only child of a doting mother and grandmother living under the same roof. Both women made sure he had the finest clothes for every occasion. The women quickly replaced his clothes once they no longer fit.

Harlan was the center of attention and was rarely denied his wishes. His mother and grandmother were crazy in love with the boy and ready to spoil him at all costs. Their love intensified when Harlan was five years old.

He came home from kindergarten on a snowy December 16th day in Warren, Ohio. The walk was cold, but that wasn't unusual given the time of year. Only three more days of school for the youngster before school let out for the two-week Christmas break.

The weatherman predicted this day to be the first significant snowfall of the year. Harlan couldn't wait to play in the snow.

His father promised him that morning they would build a snowman if the forecast were correct. The five inches of snowfall appeared to be well on its way; Harlan couldn't wait to get home. The handsome little boy passed multiple snowball fights to ensure he was home and ready for his dad once he walked through the door. The only thing better than time with Dad was the anticipation of Santa Claus, and that was just around the corner.

Dudley Marks was a conscientious man if nothing else. He was well-respected at the mill, and his managers were grooming him for further advancement. He was now the quality manager for the steel mill responsible for incoming inspections. It wasn't uncommon for him to stay later than expected each day as he poured over tests and calculations to ensure reliability.

However, today was different. He took a half-day vacation. He needed to leave by lunch to be home before his son arrived home. The snow already began to fall.

Dudley finished his scheduled morning meeting and inspections before he sat down at his desk. As Dudley gathered himself, he became short of breath. His chest locked up as the pain became more severe. Dudley couldn't cry out for help as his lungs starved for oxygen. Each gasp for air became shorter and shorter. He was suffocating, and he didn't know why. He placed his head on his desk. Within moments the pain began to fade, but so did Dudley Marks.

A co-worker thought Dudley was reaching for a pencil that had fallen to the floor when he noticed something more urgent – Dudley wasn't moving.

The 38-year-old man was gone.

A week earlier, Dudley hit his leg squarely on a board, stored on the front porch, that caused a deep bruise. Two sleepless nights later, he went to his doctor when the bruise on his shin continued to swell.

"Give it time. I know it hurts, but it will pass. You're going to live to be 100 years old, don't worry," was all the doctor had to say.

The call came. Martha Marks dropped the phone and could only scream in terror while her elder mother tried to make sense of what happened. Nan grabbed her daughter by the shoulders and spun her around. Now, standing face-to-face, she knew. Her daughter's future was shattered.

A few hours later, Harlan Marks arrived home early. He was able to shave five minutes from his walk due to his excitement.

Walking in the door on any given school day was always a treat. Nan always had a chocolate snack, and hugs and kisses were abundant from Grandma and Mom, even though he pretended not to like them.

Harlan bounced on to the porch and slammed his shoulder against the front door that always stuck in the cold weather. He pulled off his boots as he looked around the living room to see no one there to greet him.

He heard multiple footsteps race briskly through the hall, and he saw his mother coming to embrace him. Harlan noticed no smiles. His mother looked very sad, and Harlan became frightened. Martha held her son tight kneeling on the ground with him at shoulder level. She buried her head behind his, and although he couldn't see her face, he heard the uncontrollable sobs.

Nan was standing in front of him. He could see her face clearly, and he knew she was crying. Out of fear, Harlan began to cry. He had never witnessed his strong mother or grandmother cry before, and if they were upset, so was he.

It was later determined that Dudley Marks died from a pulmonary embolism. The bruise in his leg formed a clot that broke loose and traveled through the bloodstream into the lungs. The clot lodged in a smaller lung artery creating a blockage to the heart.

Life would never be the same for Dudley's five-year-old boy. The snowman was never built.

TWELVE

"The light of the righteous shines brightly,
but the lamp of the wicked is snuffed out."

VICTORIA MARKS NEVER HEARD THE AUTHORITIES SCRAMBLE TO attention when her husband returned to the house. The frenzied agents were so desperate to apprehend Harlan they almost forgot to keep someone to watch over the 48-year-old woman.

It wasn't difficult for the two remaining agents to assess that Victoria wasn't fully alert. The agents tried to speak to her, but she was unresponsive. She was in a catatonic state after breaking down. Her mental capacity was void of comprehension, and Victoria was slipping into a state of shock.

The house was now empty and in a state of disarray. Victoria remained on the floor with her hands cuffed behind her back. Her eyes gazed into the distance – she could not speak a word.

The agents removed the handcuffs once they recognized the seriousness of the situation. Victoria's skin was getting cold, and she began to shake uncontrollably. One agent went to the living room, grabbed a blanket from the couch, and wrapped it around her shoulders.

"We need to get this woman to a hospital immediately," one shouted to the other.

A prideful woman since her marriage to Harlan, Victoria didn't grow up that way. She was number nine in a family of 11 children growing up in Anderson, IN. Her Catholic upbringing prepared each sibling for a life devoted to God. It was only Victoria who would turn away from the church.

Her parents were hard-working teachers and Victoria, along with six other siblings, chose the same career. She was the quiet one in the family, although she didn't lack confidence. Victoria was smart but used her time in large groups as an observer more than a participant.

Victoria had an innate ability to compartmentalize each situation, regardless if it was good or bad. Her emotional pendulum didn't swing too far in either direction. She was always steady and didn't care to share her feelings with anyone, which often concerned her parents. Most people quickly concluded that she was cold and unfriendly. Victoria knew how others felt about her, and she grew to embrace those characteristics.

She wanted to travel her own path following high school. Her college major was education focusing on behavioral science, which meant plenty of psychology classes.

It was a choice that shocked her parents since Victoria never wanted to have kids. They knew she was not the maternal type. They also took this to mean that she didn't like children and for the most part, they were right. However, Victoria understood her personality was authoritarian, and in the city school system it was considered a valued trait. While this wouldn't come in handy teaching Kindergarten, it was a strength if she wanted to work with older kids who were on the brink of self-destruction.

She excelled in Philosophy and Logic. Both were key to her major, and the classes came easy. While many undergraduates had difficulty grasping the concepts, Victoria found comfort in using common sense to draw conclusions. Its teaching confirmed her logic that if something couldn't be seen, felt, or heard, then it couldn't exist.

She used the same concepts to question her belief in God. It was something she struggled with during her upbringing. But, she wouldn't dare question her parents' ideals for fear of backlash. It simply wasn't worth the battle. Now she had a basis for her opinion. At least in her mind, it was reasonable to suggest God may not exist. At age 20, Victoria's only answer to whether there was a God was that she could not draw a conclusion. More hard evidence was needed, and faith alone wasn't enough. Her understanding of religion would remain dormant in her mind and her heart.

The independent co-ed didn't come home on the weekends like the other siblings. She knew going back to Anderson would mean Mass on Saturday night and again on Sunday morning. It was overkill going once, let alone twice.

When her parents came to visit her at her Ball State campus apartment, Victoria made a point to stop at St. Mary's Catholic Church and pick up a bulletin. She placed it strategically on her kitchen table for her parents to see. It pleased them greatly that their daughter was attending service although they never spoke a word. The bulletin brought her anonymity. Keeping secrets from her parents wasn't a sign of parental fear. It was out of respect to avoid hurting their feelings.

The young woman was gaining power through her self-reliance. No longer was her schedule dictated by church, her parents, or even her brothers and sisters. All decisions belonged to her. She found power in controlling her life.

Victoria was career driven and landed a job upon graduation in the Indianapolis Public School system. She continued to pursue her master's degree and then her specialist degree, both of which continued to increase her value with the school. Eventually, she began teaching kids who were diagnosed with severe behavioral handicaps. It meant they were kids who were about to get kicked out of school. Victoria was their last hope in obtaining an education. She was the only person standing between a life of crime or obtaining a high school diploma.

Not long into her career, she met a man and got married. He wasn't *Mr. Right*. He was *Mr. Right Timing*. It was part of her plan. She told him the only way this was going to work was without children. It came as no surprise for anyone who spent time with her. Growing up in a house with so many children may have soured her. Regardless, the focus for the rest of her life was on her. It was a silent rebellion she would harbor. She became nearly unapproachable for co-workers. Friends would come and go quickly once they got to know her well.

The marriage was short lived. She determined the union wasn't working, so she flipped on her bitch-switch – hoping to make her unsuspecting husband miserable. She looked forward to reaping the alimony.

The results were better than she anticipated. Victoria came home one day to find his car running in the garage and a hose duct taped from the exhaust into the car window. She was simply hoping he'd just give up and request a divorce, but this alternative would do quite nicely. It also made the paperwork and financials much easier.

Now, as she slowly opened and closed her eyes, she tried to remind herself that she was in control of her life. While the chase continued for Harlan Marks, the two agents remaining at the house quickly called an ambulance. Within five minutes the squad arrived and began assessing her. The medics asked her basic questions hoping to get a response. Victoria remained distant; her eyes blinked once and then remained wide open.

She was taken to Ascension St. Vincent Fisher's Hospital for emergency treatment and placed in the psychiatric care unit overnight for observation. After two IV bags and a Xanax later, Victoria Marks began to come around.

At first, she accepted admission to the hospital. A nurse, who remained in the room the entire time, questioned her regarding her whereabouts. Victoria was confused to learn she was in a psych ward until she recalled the chain of events.

Victoria quickly became sick to her stomach as she realized this wasn't a nightmare. It was real. The anxiety over the past 18 months was nothing compared to how she felt now. Even with the medication taking effect, the level of reality nearly caused her to faint.

Until now, Victoria was able to stave off the darkness surrounding her and Harlan. She focused on her job, social status, and the spoils that came with money. The danger signs were present, but she chose to overlook them. Victoria trusted her husband and believed that a better life was coming soon.

She felt a sudden desire to be sitting at the dinner table with her parents wishing she was 12 years old again. Her father would pull out his Bible after every meal and read from the book of Psalms. It was a tiny inconvenience for Victoria since she pretended to be interested at the time. But what she wouldn't give to go back to a simpler time. Now it was too late.

Fantasy was quickly interrupted when she heard voices shouting her name. She knew that now wasn't the time to let down her guard. She needed to be alert.

Victoria opened her eyes to find a nurse talking to her and checking her pulse. Her body was still, but she felt unsettled once again. The nurse walked out of the room, and Victoria began to fade out of consciousness until she was finally asleep for the night.

She awoke with the sun. Victoria felt dizzy but more alert. The last thing she recalled yesterday evening was a doctor telling a nurse to administer a shot to help her sleep. She spent the night in the psychiatric unit, but she felt none the better for it.

Harlan entered her mind, and she began to worry once again. She had no idea of his whereabouts or his safety.

Did he make it to the Cayman Islands? she thought. *Could he have gone without me? The authorities wouldn't allow him to board a plane. Where is he?*

She had no answers to these questions, but years of psychology told her she wouldn't learn the answers until she was discharged from the hospital.

Victoria closed her eyes and took a deep breath. She knew she needed to focus. Victoria had to solve one problem at a time, and right now she had to convince the doctors that she was well enough to be released.

Doctors came again to ask questions. This time Victoria was able to answer everything clearly and calmly. Thirty minutes of questioning proved to be a challenge since Victoria was growing impatient. She continued to remind herself of the importance of how she answered. The doctor wasn't just paying attention to her words, but also focusing on how she emotionally responded to the questions. Her cognitive thinking and emotional state convinced the good doctor she was stable. At 1 p.m. Monday the paperwork was signed, and Victoria Marks was released from care.

She considered a cab back to her home but erased that thought. She knew the agents tore the home to pieces as they tried to gather information about the case. Going home would be too painful, and she wasn't ready for that right now.

An orderly offered to escort Victoria out the door in a wheelchair.

"No," Victoria nearly shouted. "I mean, no thank you," realizing he was trying to do his job.

The orderly saw she was agitated and needed additional guidance.

"Let me take you to the service counter, and they can help you make a call."

Her cell phone was lost if not already seized by the authorities. She had no way to check messages, text, or otherwise. She didn't have a lot of options.

Victoria forced a smile. "I would appreciate that. Thank you."

She thought in that moment she must be insane. Any sane person would have emotionally shut down. She was exhausted, yet anxious.

Victoria walked with the young man to the service counter and asked to place a call. She dialed the number for Marks Management Services and asked to speak with Elaine.

Elaine Hansen was the company vice president for Harlan and Victoria. When employees needed answers, they went to Elaine rather than Harlan. Elaine knew more about the day-to-day operations than the owner. She was strong-willed with an accounting background that helped the Marks make a lot of money. Files were always orderly, and she made sure everyone under her knew their role.

"Elaine, this is Victoria."

"Victoria, where are you? Harlan didn't show up this morning, and I can't reach him. Is everything ok?"

"No, Elaine it's not. I need your help, but I don't want to talk over the phone. Please come and pick me up at St. Vincent Hospital in Fisher's as soon as you can. We're in trouble."

"Oh my God. Are you alright? Is Harlan ok?"

"Yes, we're…I mean…no, not really. Elaine, please come and pick me up. I'll explain everything."

"I'm on my way."

Elaine was well versed regarding the troubles from the Criminal Division of the IRS. In fact, Harlan asked her to gather information that was turned over to the government and, eventually Jay Hausmann. She sat through many meetings to help answer questions about the business and the Marks' financial affairs.

But this was different. Elaine was heading to the hospital and didn't know why. Victoria was unwilling to answer questions over the phone. She feared Harlan had a heart attack, and he possibly didn't survive.

Wouldn't Victoria have been crying? She seemed to have it somewhat together, Elaine thought.

Elaine said goodbye to no one as she exited the building. The hospital was 30 minutes away, but Elaine was able to arrive in twenty. The expressway was the Indianapolis Motor Speedway considering Elaine's urgency. By the time she pulled to the front of the emergency parking lot at St. Vincent, she began to experience a minor panic attack.

She was relieved to see Victoria heading out toward the car. It didn't take long to realize that Harlan was nowhere in sight. Victoria was alone. Elaine noted that Victoria had nothing in her hands, not even her purse.

"What the hell is going on?" Elaine Hansen asked abruptly.

Victoria sat down in the car and closed the door. Without looking at Victoria, she broke down once again.

"It's happened. It's happened," she repeated.

"What's happened, Victoria? What's happened?"

"They came for us. The government agents… they came for us last night and… and… I don't know … I… I can't find Harlan. I don't know where he is, and no one can tell me anything, and I'm afraid to ask." Victoria's cries turned to screams. Her voice intensified with the grim reality.

Elaine sat in stunned silence. How could this be happening?

Why would government agents come for them when they gave them all the information? It all seemed so airtight. It was all a big misunderstanding that would be resolved after a few more meetings. What went wrong? Elaine wondered.

"We'll…We'll find him, Victoria. You have to talk to me. Please calm down and tell me everything that happened."

"They found out. Somehow the authorities found out we were going to leave the country. How did they know?"

Elaine couldn't believe her ears. Did Victoria Marks just say she and Harlan were going to leave the country? If Elaine Hansen knew one thing, she knew fleeing the country wasn't something Harlan had shared.

THIRTEEN

"The house of the righteous contains great treasure,
but the income of the wicked bring them trouble."

Harlan Marks gathered himself in the hotel lobby. He knew he was experiencing everything for the last time. On this sunny, fall Monday morning Jay Hausmann's black Audi pulled next to the door to pick up his client. Harlan, with no belongings, took a deep breath to calm his nerves.

As if he were preparing to go on a Sunday drive, Harlan sat inside the car, buckled the seat belt, and stared straight ahead in silence.

Hausmann didn't budge except to stare at his client.

"What the hell were you thinking!" Hausmann nearly shouted. It wasn't a question but a dumbfounded expression. "You have complicated this case for yourself and me. You look guilty as hell for running last night."

Harlan said nothing and didn't glance toward his driver and attorney. It was as if he heard nothing at all. In many ways, that was true. Harlan was too fixated on what was going to happen next. Besides, there wasn't anything that Jay Hausmann could say that he didn't already tell himself a hundred times.

The trip to the downtown firm of Fisher, Comer & Scarffe seemed long, but Harlan didn't complain. It would be a while before he could ride in a luxury vehicle, so he treasured the moment. In many ways, this particular ride was more appreciated than the Emirates Airline he and Victoria flew to Dubai. It was even more appreciated and comfortable than the elite seven-star hotel, Burj Al Arab Jumeirah, which included a host of private butlers costing a reasonable $1,360 per night.

Hausmann used the time to tell Harlan the due process and protocol that would take place once they arrived at the downtown firm. Harlan was partially paying attention but mostly his mind was on Victoria.

Harlan managed one significant thought. Victoria wouldn't be surprised, but this was without question, going to make the newspaper if it already hadn't.

"Am I the front-page news this morning?" he asked.

"Not yet. That will come tomorrow once the authorities find out you're in custody. You were the headliner last night on the police scanner, but it didn't get any further. Get ready. It's coming, and it's coming full steam."

Harlan knew it was true, but he didn't want to hear it out loud. It made it too real. Everything was becoming too real. It was *so real* that Harlan finally realized he couldn't make it go away by avoiding the thought. It was here to stay.

The two arrived at the firm. As Hausmann escorted Harlan into his office, the other employees in the firm couldn't help but stare. They knew what was about to go down, and although they understood Harlan Marks had done wrong, they could only take pity on him. Harlan felt the stares and resented each and every one.

"Get used to it," Hausmann quipped as he picked up his client's non-verbal cues.

He escorted Harlan into his office and closed the door behind him.

"Do you know what is going to happen today?" asked the attorney. "Did you hear anything I said to you in the car?"

"No, I'm sorry I didn't."

It was the first time the counselor heard Harlan Marks apologize for anything.

"I'll explain it to you one more time. I know your mind is going a million miles an hour. However, I'm going to be with you every step of the way."

"Are you going to be in the jail cell with me?" Harlan asked sarcastically.

Hausmann didn't respond to the question. He shared the likely events that would take place the remainder of the day.

"I'm about to place a call to David Costello, but before I do, is there anything you need me to do?"

"Why wouldn't you just take me to the jail for booking?" Marks inquired.

"Protocol," said Hausmann. "As an attorney, common courtesy is to contact your counterpart. Trust me, I can't stand the government authorities any more than you, but I also know that Costello and Spawn will hold a grudge if I by-pass their authority. Also, I want Costello to know that you turned yourself in and did the right thing. You didn't try to flee the country as they thought. I'm hoping that could earn us some bonus points."

Hausmann continued after a long pause. "Again, is there anything I can do for you before we get started with all the fun?"

"I need you to get in touch with my wife. She has to be wondering where I am or if I'm still alive."

"I tried to do that on the way to pick you up, but her cell phone didn't answer. I found out through sources that she was taken to St. Vincent Hospital overnight for observation after having an emotional breakdown. When I found that out, I figured we could contact her later."

"Did you try to reach Elaine Hansen to share anything?"

"Keep in mind, Harlan, that you are my client. No one else. Everything that I know is confidential between you and me. By the letter of my oath, I never should have tried to contact Victoria."

"OK," was all Harlan could say as his lips began to quiver, and tears began to slide steadily down his face.

Jay Hausmann stepped out of the office. When he returned, he handed Harlan a cup of coffee.

"I just asked my secretary to get Costello on the phone. It shouldn't take long. I'm sure he'll answer the call," Hausmann smiled slightly.

Harlan found the humor and gave a courtesy laugh.

Within seconds the secretary notified her boss, "Mr. Hausmann, Sir, I have Mr. Costello on the phone."

The two men shared momentary eye contact as they recognized the importance of what was about to happen.

"Here we go," said Hausmann.

Harlan couldn't hear the conversation from the other side of the phone. He didn't need to hear. Jay Hausmann laid out the current circumstance to Costello and told him that Harlan Marks was now in his office and prepared to turn himself over to the authorities. The conversation was less than five minutes long, with Hausmann doing most of the talking.

Hausmann arranged to privately turn his client over to avoid cameras, reporters, and other news outlets. From the conversation, Harlan gathered that the federal agents would come to the Fisher, Comer & Scarffe office.

Jay Hausmann hung up the phone and didn't need to relay the message, but he did so anyway.

"They will be here in about 20 minutes. I can't tell if Costello is going to drive downtown or do cartwheels all the way here. He is angry about what happened last night, but also relieved. Your escape, as Costello called it, turned out to be a very embarrassing situation for Spawn and his agency. I asked him if we could meet him at the prison, but he refused. He's grand-standing and wants his 15 minutes of fame. We'll give it to him. Not that we have a choice. I did insist that we do this quietly, and he agreed. We'll see if he keeps his end of the bargain."

"What happens next?" Harlan requested.

"Well, the Grand Jury will meet. You will be indicted. The criminal investigators were aware of your plan to flee the country. That would have been something I would have liked to have known myself," Hausmann said scolding his client.

Harlan went numb. "How did they know?" he asked under his breath but loud enough for Hausmann to hear.

"Are you kidding me? I guess you've been funneling money to whatever location you were slipping off to, and most likely, you have your eye on a property if you haven't already purchased real estate. Please tell me that you didn't purchase any property. Please, Harlan. Please, at least tell me that didn't happen."

Harlan Marks didn't look up and could only nod his head, which confirmed Hausmann's suspicions.

"Oh, Jesus Christ. How the hell am I supposed to defend you, Harlan? We had a fighter's chance before all this!" Hausmann exclaimed. "Do you have any idea how you elevated this case? Harlan, you just made yourself the government poster boy. They will mount your head above the fireplace of their Criminal Hall of Fame. You handed them the easiest victory they've seen in years."

A deep sigh by Jay Hausmann allowed him a moment to calm down. He reminded himself this wasn't the first white-collar case he defended. But now, the situation went from quiet and concealed to becoming the largest Medicare fraud case in the Tri-State area, and possibly, the United States.

"Where in God's green acre were you planning to go anyway?"

"The Cayman Islands," Harlan Marks whispered holding back more tears.

Hausmann paused, realizing he didn't have much more time with his client.

"The Judge was also made aware of your plan to escape and granted the warrant sometime last week. You will likely be charged with a multitude of crimes, especially after you ran from the authorities last night. It's a laundry list of convictions; I'm sure. They have been ahead of you the whole time. It all looks bad for our defense."

"I'm sure Spawn has been tracking all your actions. I'm guessing you also purchased airline tickets to the Cayman Islands, which would have been the final straw. They knew you were leaving once you started sending money to a foreign bank and purchased property. They just didn't know when. Once the airline tickets were in hand, your timeline was a dead giveaway. They went to the judge and made a case that you needed to be apprehended immediately. The judge agreed."

Without pause, Hausmann asked his client, "So, Harlan, how am I doing so far?" He didn't wait for a response.

Hausmann told Harlan that he would be held overnight and not hold out hope for bond since he attempted to leave the country.

"There will be an initial appearance, likely tomorrow. It's an arraignment. We will ask for you to be let out on bond, but the judge won't allow it so don't get your hopes up for that either. After they read the list of crimes that you have been charged with, we will plead not guilty. I'll get a list of the charges before the hearing and hopefully have a moment alone to go over those with you.

Jay Hausmann thought about the events last night and laughed at Spawn's misfortune. "How in the hell did you get away from so many agents and police anyway?" he chuckled.

Hausmann didn't expect an answer, and Harlan Marks wasn't about to give it to him.

The late morning sun now beamed warmly on Harlan Marks through the large floor to ceiling window in Hausmann's office. It was growing too hot to sit in its direct path, but Harlan wasn't about to move.

He now placed a value on simple things that stimulated the five senses. The touch of a comfortable bed, the smell of a fresh-cut lawn, the sound of waves beating lightly against his sailboat, the taste of a St. Elmo steak, and most importantly, the sight of his beautiful wife were enjoyments he could no longer take for granted but were part of a distant past.

Hausmann had nothing more to say to his client. He also recognized Harlan's moment of reflection and allowed him some time.

It happens to the best of them, especially when it comes to white-collar clients, Hausmann thought.

It's what Hausmann referred to as the "moment of transition." It's the time when individuals stop fighting and have no more tears to shed. Terminally ill patients experience it as well. They finally accept their reality and begin to experience a calming effect. What's going to be will be, and there's a sense of relief that the pain is over.

His thoughts were interrupted when the phone rang in Hausmann's office. The sound startled Harlan, bringing him out of his meditation. Hausmann wasn't ready either. He sprang from his chair and hit the speaker button.

"Mr. Costello has arrived with Agent Spawn," his secretary stated.

"OK, we're on our way down. Tell them we will meet them in the lobby," and then disconnected.

"It's time, Harlan."

Jay Hausmann walked his client out of the office and down the hall toward the elevator. Hausmann placed his arm around Harlan's shoulder and could feel the pain his client was experiencing.

He wasn't about to tell him it was going to get worse before it got better. The media would find out, and the news would soon dominate the airwaves, newspapers, and all social outlets. Family members had yet to find out. As well, the Marion County Jail wasn't a place for the weak.

The elevator door opened, and Harlan Marks never looked up. Spawn was wearing a big smile to go along with his cheap suit. Costello greeted the attorney first, then Spawn addressed Harlan.

"Mr. Mark's, you have the right to remain silent when questioned. Anything you say or do may be used against you in a court of law. You have the right to consult an attorney before speaking to the police and to have an attorney present during questioning now or in the future. Do you understand?"

"Yes."

"If you cannot afford one, one will be appointed for you before any questioning if you wish. Do you understand?

"Yes."

With that, Agent Spawn experienced the highlight of his day, week, and maybe his year.

"Turn around and place your hands behind your back."

Harlan cooperated and turned his back to the agent. Spawn snapped the handcuffs across Harlan Marks wrists and snugged them extra tight, causing his prisoner to wince in pain. Grabbing him by the forearm, he led Marks to the awaiting car. Still, Harlan never bothered to look up.

FOURTEEN

"Wisdom is supreme; therefore get wisdom.
Though it cost all you have, get understanding."

5:30 ON A TUESDAY MORNING CAME EARLY FOR CLAIRE AND HARRISON as they prepared for the workday. The nights were getting shorter for Claire as she entered the end of her second trimester. Early mornings were difficult. Truth be told, the nights were also short for Harrison as it was difficult for him to sleep. However, he was too smart to say anything regarding the matter.

Harrison always encouraged Claire to get up first since she took the longest. He often joked he could be ready to go to the moon in less than 10 minutes. Plus, it allowed him an extra 20 minutes of necessary sleep. Even the king size bed wasn't big enough to avoid Claire's wrath during the midnight hours. It became so bad that the dog even started to sleep on the floor. Once Claire got out of bed, Zoe jumped in and curled up next to Harrison. Both could now have a few minutes of peace.

Claire never referred to herself as a morning person, but once she climbed out of bed, she became the angel with whom Harrison fell in love. She closed the bathroom door and immediately turned on the radio to listen to music and local news.

As she prepped for her shower, she turned the volume up so she could sing along to the top hits of the week. Claire was a self-described singer who thought she had perfect pitch. Harrison wasn't so convinced, but he loved listening to her enthusiasm as she oscillated from a high note to low. Although not a great singer, she was at least entertaining.

Harrison forced himself out of his slumber when he heard his cell phone ring.

Who needs me at 6 a.m.? he thought as he sat up from his warm bed to reach across the nightstand.

"Hello?" Harrison asked without checking the caller I.D.

He thought it was Mimi on the other end, but it didn't sound like her. He heard panic and urgency in her voice that was too difficult to comprehend.

Harrison snapped to attention as he knew something was desperately wrong. She was an old lady living by herself, and she could be calling him as a last measure seeking help.

Did she fall? Is she having a heart attack? he wondered with worry.

He asked her to calm down and speak slowly. "Please, Mimi. Tell me what you just said. Help me understand."

At that same time, Claire opened the bathroom door and stood motionless. Her eyes were wide, and fear crippled her face. She wanted to say something to Harrison, but the words couldn't come out. She could only stare at her husband as she watched his expression change to disbelief and complete shock.

"Have you seen the newspaper this morning?" his grandmother asked.

"No, Mimi. Why?"

"Your dad is on the front page. He's been arrested. It's a whole article. Oh, Harrison. I don't know what I'm going to do. I wish I were dead."

Mimi continued talking, but Harrison heard nothing after she mentioned arrest.

"Wait, wait. What did you just say? He's been arrested?" Harrison tried to ask knowing this couldn't be true.

He shook his head and blinked hard, trying to pull himself from this wretched nightmare, but the tactic wasn't working.

He looked at Claire, hoping to find safety in her expression. Maybe she could wake him from his terrible nightmare.

She was trying to comprehend something of her own. Claire had just heard the morning news blaring from her portable radio. Harlan Marks had been arrested and charged with Medicare fraud and money laundering.

"Harrison. Harrison. Are you there? Can you hear me?" Mimi was now shouting into the phone. She needed someone to fix this, and Harrison was her only hope.

He eventually heard the cries of his grandmother and acknowledged that he was still on the line.

"Yes, I'm here," was all Harrison could mutter.

"Can you please come over? I need to see you. Please come over as soon as you can."

"OK. I'll be there as soon as I can."

He slowly put down the phone and stared emotionless at his pregnant wife.

He went to his laptop and pulled up the local news. He only needed to click once to see the picture of his father plastered on the front page. A long article surrounded the 3x5 picture with the headline, *Firm's Owner Held Over Medicare Fraud.*

Harrison gazed at the screen. He couldn't bring himself to read the details. His mind would not allow him to process what he was seeing – was this actually his father?

Claire placed her hand on her husband's shoulder to offer comfort. Harrison was startled, not realizing she was standing next to him.

"What does it say?" she asked reluctantly.

"I don't know."

Harrison knew he had to read the article. As much as he didn't want to, he was a person that needed answers quickly – no matter if they were good or bad. He was a problem solver, and the only way to solve a problem is to learn the details.

This was not one of those times. He forced himself to read aloud.

"The owner of Marks Medical Supply, Inc., and other related companies, was arrested yesterday because federal agents, following a money trail, believe he was about to flee the country."

Harrison's body went numb, and he felt a pit at the bottom of his stomach. He convinced himself to continue.

"Harlan Marks, 56, of Fishers, IN, has been charged with money laundering, mail fraud, and conspiracy in an alleged scheme to defraud Medicare of $15.5 million. He surrendered to federal agents after his house and autos were searched in a raid conducted Sunday night.

In an affidavit unsealed yesterday in U.S. District Court, Andrew Spawn, an Internal Revenue Service special agent, stated the alleged scheme was based primarily on the sale to nursing homes of adult diapers and undergarments.

Although those items aren't covered by the federal insurance agency, the affidavit states that nursing homes and individual Medicare beneficiaries were told their claims would be paid. Mr. Mark's company allegedly submitted claims describing the items supplied as devices which are covered by the insurance."

Harrison began to read silently now as he was having trouble consuming the information.

The article explained that government documents claimed approximately 98 percent of the company's total gross receipts over four years were from illegal billing.

The younger Marks learned details from the article they wouldn't have suspected. They knew Harlan was capable of some questionable business deals, but this was beyond their imagination.

They had no idea Harlan and Victoria had purchased property in the Cayman Islands, although they knew they made many trips.

But most importantly, Harrison's dad was in jail and it wasn't just he and Claire that knew.

"The whole city is now aware of this, Claire," Harrison stated.

She mentioned as calmly as she could, trying not to further upset her husband, "Before the end of the day, the whole country will know."

He thought for a moment before he responded. Claire certainly had a point. The news was much bigger than Indianapolis, Indiana. News will travel through the state of Indiana and at the very least, the tri-state area.

The article cited it was the biggest Medicare scheme in the Midwest, and Harrison was just getting to that part.

"This is going to be on every news channel and newspaper in Indiana," Harrison stated as he realized the impact. "This might even make the national news."

He sank slowly onto the bed. There was no possible way he could stand up. At this point in their lives, the younger couple should be celebrating as he and Claire expected their first child. Thanksgiving and Christmas were just months away. There would be no celebrating this year. Harlan Marks just took it all away.

Claire kneeled on the floor next to him. She placed her head on his lap and cried. He bent over drawing his head close to hers and kissed her head softly.

"I'm sorry. I'm so sorry, Claire."

Harrison felt his eyes well up but tried to blink away the tears. He expected no response from Claire, and that's exactly what he got. Their future plans were in jeopardy. The outcome was unclear. The only certainty was uncertainty and the fact that they would have to face co-workers, friends, neighbors and other family members who would want to know the details.

Finally Harrison looked at the clock. It was 7:30 a.m. and Claire was going to be late for work. She was determined to go. She knew her absence would be worse than facing the office staff.

She would need to figure out how to deal with co-workers that purposely ignored the topic or stopped her in the hallway to ask questions. There were at least three employees that lived in one of the many apartments owned and operated by Marks Management Service, Inc.

Claire kissed her husband and bolted for the door, wiping her eyes along the way.

Harrison realized he promised his grandmother a visit, and he was running behind. His cell phone rang, and it was her calling to find out where he had been. She was struggling and needed his undivided attention.

He didn't bother to answer. The best he could do was make the drive to her home, which was also a property owned and operated by his father.

"Oh, Jesus." Harrison came to realize. "Everyone in that complex knows who she is and will be ringing her doorbell once they hear the news."

He soon understood why she needed him as soon as possible. The other residents had no class when it came to giving people their space.

Harrison realized that he had a customer golf outing today with his sales manager, who was traveling from Chicago. They were supposed to meet in Zionsville at 10 a.m.

He could still make that happen. He got dressed, threw his clubs in his vehicle, and headed toward her apartment. He needed to calm her and get his emotions in check.

During the 15 minute-drive, he took time to clear his mind. Growing up as an only child in the country, he was used to consoling himself. When his parents weren't getting along before the divorce, he would retreat to the barn's hay loft to be alone. The escape proved to be an effective self-defense mechanism to block those from the outside. It gave him the space he needed to resolve problems and remind himself everything would be alright.

Now was very much like the time he was a kid. At 15 years old, he thought his parent's divorce was the worst thing that could happen. And today, Harrison had no idea he would be dealing with his father's federal crime that could capture the nation's attention.

Harrison reminded himself again that everything was going to be ok. He and Claire had a strong marriage, a house, and of course a baby on the way. He still had his mom and his step-dad, and Claire's parents. Her parents were also there to offer their undying support.

When he arrived at his grandmother's apartment, the apartment manager was there to greet him. She knew Harrison well and heard the news. He and Claire paid regular visits to see his grandmother and always made a point to share a smile and wave. He was certainly no stranger. Being well known often had privileges most days. Today was not that day.

Harrison nodded his head toward her and she knew this was not the time for questions.

Skipping the elevator, Harrison took the stairs to reach the 2nd floor. He knocked on Mimi's door. She opened right away and scolded him for being tardy.

"Where have you been?"

Harrison was not surprised. He even chuckled at her response.

"Look, Mimi. I heard the news for the first time when you called this morning. I've spent the morning reading and re-reading the article to try and understand it all."

"Oh, Harrison. I don't know what to do. I don't know what happened. I don't know anything. People around here are calling and knocking on my door. They want to know what's going on, and I don't know what to tell them. Even if I did know, I just want to be left alone. I can't even go outside."

Harrison told her more information would come out. He promised her he would talk to Elaine. She was going to be his biggest resource and would know everything that was going on.

"You've got to give me some time to ask some questions, Mimi. Will you give me time?" Harrison knew she had no choice but to grant his request. What else was a 90 year old woman to do?

FIFTEEN

"Penalties are prepared for mockers,
and beatings for the backs of fools."

THE CONVERSATION WITH ELAINE HANSEN DIDN'T GO AS EXPECTED. By now she was aware Harlan turned himself over to authorities and made it a priority to bring herself up to speed since she picked Victoria up from the hospital a day earlier. Besides, it was her job to know these things, and it was her responsibility to keep the company running until her boss returned.

When Harrison entered his dad's company he had no intention of stopping at the front desk. He walked directly past the young receptionist without glancing. Normally he would have followed protocol and waited politely in the lobby. Today was not normal.

The receptionist wasn't about to stop the owner's son, who looked like he was on a mission. Fortunately for her, Elaine was standing within view of Harrison and greeted him before the young lady had to respond. Elaine guided Harrison to her office, which was situated next to his father's corner suite.

"This is all a mistake, Harrison. Your dad is going to be out before the end of the day. Don't worry. And by the way, don't listen to anything the media is saying. They have no idea what they are talking about."

Elaine started her version of the story from the time she picked up Victoria to when the media broke the news that morning.

Harrison couldn't help but chuckle when he learned Victoria was in the mental ward, but even that was difficult surrounding the other turmoil.

The young man wanted to believe his dad would soon be released, but it was difficult to convince himself otherwise. It wasn't too often if ever, federal agents made a mistake arresting someone. When the government makes an arrest it typically means they have been involved for several months. Harrison knew that his arrest wasn't a mistake in identity.

He wasn't feeling any better about the situation when he left. Elaine was delusional with blind devotion to her boss.

Harrison had one phone call left to make.

Benton Jeffers handled all the business legalities for Harlan Marks. Harrison thought Jeffers could give him the real story. He knew his father trusted Benton with everything.

Harrison left the building and immediately dialed Jeffers' office. The secretary put him through to the attorney so quickly Harrison wondered if his father's attorney was expecting this call.

"Harrison," the somber voice on the other end of the phone confirmed. "What are your plans today?"

Harrison's phone call was no surprise to Jeffers.

"I don't know," Harrison stumbled even though he knew he had a customer golf outing scheduled. "What the hell is going on?"

"I know this is very confusing for you, but here's what I can tell you. Your dad is definitely in trouble. He has a hearing today at 3:30. Although I am not representing your dad in his criminal defense, I will still be there for support. Think you can make the hearing? He needs your support."

"OK," was all Harrison could add.

Jeffers went on, "After the hearing, I would like you to come to my office. You and I can talk."

"OK. I guess I'll see you at 3:30," he replied, barely able to put a sentence together.

Harrison knew, however, that he had to meet his boss for the customer golf outing. He was going to have to decline a fun-filled day of golf. The only way to get out of this responsibility was to come clean with the truth. Harrison's difficult day became more stressful.

When Harrison arrived at Darrin's Coffee Company to meet his boss, he looked down at his watch. He arrived ahead of schedule and thought about how to break the news to Howard. Harrison didn't want his boss to view him unfavorably. Even more, he wasn't prepared to have a conversation about a topic he still didn't understand.

He read the article again while he waited for his boss. Strategically, Harrison walked out of his grandmother's apartment with the newspaper in hand so she couldn't obsess over the story. That decision proved to be beneficial in more ways than one.

He read the story twice again to process the information. He knew this was going to take some time, but time wasn't in his favor.

Harrison was still shaken when Howard arrived. He was a good man and intently listened as Harrison broke the story and placed the newspaper in front of him.

Howard picked up the paper and said, "You need to go. I'll take care of the customer."

"Thank you, Howard. Thank you so much."

Harrison left Howard behind and drove off. He wasn't sure where he was going, but he knew he had to keep moving.

All morning his phone rang. Both his grandmother and now his mother wanted to know what was going on. Harrison wasn't ready to talk. They would have to wait.

While driving, Harrison thought about Claire. He was worried about her. To make matters worse for her, she didn't have the information that he had uncovered in the last three hours. He had to call.

"Hey, pretty lady," he greeted her.

"I'm not so pretty right now. I've been crying in my office with the door closed. Do you know anything more?"

"Yes, I do."

He filled her in on the conversations and the plans for later that day. She offered to come to the hearing, but Harrison didn't want her to be present.

"Let me handle it. I don't know what to expect. I promise to fill you in when I get home."

Harrison sensed relief in her voice. He told her everything was going to be ok and didn't involve either one of them. He knew that saying this out loud would comfort Claire. Their lives would move forward regardless of this obstacle.

Throughout the day, Harrison kept busy by listening to local talk radio. Every commercial break led with the capture of his father, a prominent businessman in the Indianapolis area.

He also turned on the television to catch the local news at noon. The three major networks led with the story just as he expected.

Harrison was suddenly overcome with emotion as if a small wave gained momentum, took him by surprise and slammed him onto the shore. Seeing his father's mug shot on television over and over was more than he could handle. He broke down.

"What the hell is going on?" he screamed.

All he could do was ask *why*. He knew his father was a prickly person from the outside, but Harrison never imagined his dad was capable of criminal activity.

Harrison began to feel the pressure of being Harlan Marks' son more now than ever. Many people knew his father and, as a result, many people knew him too. Even the community of Hidden Shores would never be able to look at him the same. They all knew his dad. Harlan made a few friends but just as many enemies in the small lake community.

Harrison was still working hard to overcome his last name.

What will they say? How will they act? Those questions and more circulated in his head over and over as tears fell from his face.

Soon it was time to head downtown. Once he arrived at the courthouse, Harrison experienced nervous energy. He made a stop in the courthouse restroom to gather himself. He splashed water on his face and looked in the mirror.

"I can do this," he whispered.

He mounted his hands on each side of the sink and squeezed. His head was bowed down with his chin to his chest. Harrison's eyes were tightly closed.

Then he whispered, "God are you there. If there is anything you can do to help me through this moment...Please! Are you there?"

It was then Harrison smelled smoke coming from one of the bathroom stalls.

They allow smoking in the bathrooms, especially in a courthouse, he thought to himself.

At that time, a tall, slender man came out of the stall with a cigarette in hand.

"Hi," the elder gentlemen grumbled when he realized he had been caught.

"Hey," Harrison responded.

The man in the suit rubbed his cigarette out using the bottom of his shoe and threw it in the toilet.

There was only one explanation that could justify this man's arrogance.

"Are you by chance Jay Hausmann?" Harrison asked just before the man exited the bathroom.

"Yes, I am. And who are you, may I ask?" Hausmann responded curiously.

"Harrison Marks. I'm Harlan's son."

"Ahh," Hausmann groaned.

He wasn't expecting this encounter, but he knew the young man wanted answers.

"Your name was in the newspaper this morning," Harrison uttered before Hausmann could say any more. "Please tell me; how bad is it?"

"We've got our work cut out for us. I will say this, though. We've got a pretty reasonable judge assigned to the case, which should help."

"Is he going to prison? Is he going to prison for a long time?"

"Not if I can help it," Jay Hausmann said puffing out his chest.

"Now, I've got to get in that courtroom. We're going to do the best we can."

Harrison was left alone in the courthouse bathroom. He saw only his reflection to keep him company. Harrison barely recognized himself.

After a few splashes of water, Harrison dried his face and found his way to the courtroom. Benton Jeffers was already seated and motioned to him to join him.

The proceedings were about to begin, but Harrison was emotionally unprepared for what was to come next.

His father was the last person to enter the courtroom. His hands were cuffed and hung below his expanded stomach. Shackles clanked around his ankles. His walk was more of a shuffle as he wore prison appointed slippers that were too big.

Harlan also donned a brown prison jump-suit, that looked two sizes too big since it draped on his body like a growing little boy who needed his new winter pajamas to last the entire season. The only recognizable possession his father had was the glasses that sat crooked on his face.

It caught Harrison by surprise as he felt Jeffers place a hand on his shoulder to help him settle. The most disturbing reality choked him up when their eyes met for the first time. His father's sadness was obvious on his face.

Harrison never thought he would see this side of his dad. A once proud man was now reduced to public shame, and it was only going to get worse.

All the accolades he achieved in the community were now only a reminder of how hard the mighty can fall. His reign was ending abruptly. Harlan began to wish his fame and fortune never came true. He recalled a saying that his grandmother used every once in a while: "Be careful what you wish for; you just might get it." Those words were so true right now.

Harrison Marks felt his body shake. He took a couple of deep breaths to gain control and composure.

His father could only glance as he walked past, but there was nothing Harlan could do to help this loyal son. It broke Harlan's heart more than anything else that happened in the last 48 hours. He wanted so badly to reach out and hug his only child. Something he should have done so many times before but never did. It was a hopeless feeling for both.

The proceedings began with an opening statement by the U.S. Assistant Attorney, David Costello. He recapped the reason for investigating Harlan Marks and shared detailed information about the defendant laundering money to the Cayman Islands and his plan to flee the country with his wife, Victoria.

Costello elaborately told the story of Harlan's escape from federal officers only two days earlier. He pleaded that, "...no way should Harlan Marks be considered for bail."

He explained Harlan was a flight risk, and Costello wanted everyone in the courtroom to know it.

There was little that Jay Hausmann could do to convince the judge that his client would stay in Indianapolis while awaiting trial. Harlan Marks already proved otherwise.

Hausmann knew this hearing was a minor battle in a larger fight, and one that he knew he would likely lose. His effort to tell the court that Harlan did eventually turn himself in was a feeble attempt considering his client only did so when he ran out of options.

The court proceedings were over in a short time. Bail was denied, and Harlan Marks remained in custody at the Marion County Jail until trial. His trial date would be determined at the next hearing.

The judge's gavel hit hard upon the bench echoing in Harrison's ears. Harlan Marks was helped to his feet then turned to walk out of the courtroom. As Harlan turned, he looked at Harrison the entire time. As he began to walk past his son seated in the front row, Harlan stopped. The escorting police officers allowed a brief moment between father and son. A man that Harrison had never seen cry was now sobbing with his head on his shoulder.

"I'm sorry. I'm so sorry," Harlan repeated.

The pain on his face was evident, and he couldn't contain himself any longer.

Surprisingly, Harrison found strength where he thought it didn't exist. "It's going to be ok. We'll get through this. I love you, Dad."

The police pulled Harlan away and escorted him back to the jail.

Harrison was left standing while the courtroom emptied. The young man looked uncertain as he looked at Jeffers for emotional support.

"What just happened?" Harrison muttered.

"Exactly what I thought was going to happen," Jeffers responded trying to soften the situation. "Let's go back to my office. I'm not far."

Harrison didn't remember the walk from the courthouse to the office. He didn't know if it was a five-minute walk or a 20-minute walk, and he sure couldn't recall the directions. He must have followed Jeffers the entire time because now they were both sitting in a dark, cramped room with decrepit furniture, circa 1988.

He knew the kind of money that Jeffers pulled. Harrison knew what he earned for representing his father, let alone the other clients. Harrison would have thought some of the earnings from the up-and-coming attorney could have gone to hire an interior decorator.

"Excuse the mess," Jeffers said as he tried to get Harrison's attention.

"No worries."

"I know you have a lot going on right now, Harrison, and it's all very normal," Jeffers offered.

There's nothing normal about this, Harrison thought quietly.

"I think you deserve to know how it got to this point and what's about to come."

Harrison nodded in agreement.

"This investigation has been taking place for approximately two years. Your father's medical business began billing Medicare and Medicaid many years ago for products that technically weren't reimbursable."

Harrison was aware documents were handed to the government 18 months ago. Elaine Hansen let it slip while Harrison was waiting in her office to see his father on another unscheduled visit. When he asked his father about it, Harlan told him that it was a misunderstanding and that the federal government and his attorney were addressing it. It was alarming to Harrison at the time, but he never heard anything more. Elaine caught hell from Harlan for sharing the information with his son.

"I'm familiar with the circumstances, but I thought it went away. I never heard any more about it. When I asked my dad, he said it was all behind him. Is this a continuation of the same story?"

"Yes, of course. Your father is accused of selling adult diapers, creams, gauze pads, and other products to nursing homes."

And? What's wrong with that? Harrison wondered.

Jeffers continued, "Although those items aren't covered by the federal insurance agency, nursing homes and individual Medicare beneficiaries were told their claims would be paid. Your dad submitted claims describing the items as if insurance would cover each product."

Jeffers paused a moment to allow the information to register. Harrison nodded along.

"Your dad purchased the adult diapers for as little as $.45 to $.65 each and billed Medicare carriers as much as $22.57 for a single diaper."

"Oh my God. That's fraud," Harrison said with a look of distraught.

"Yes. But it gets worse," Jeffers went on. "Once your father turned in the documents and the investigation began, the Criminal Division of the IRS instructed him to cease and desist. Unfortunately, he refused and continued billing," Jeffers said with a look of disappointment.

"To him, he was following government guidelines, and that was their problem, not his. However, you and I both know the government isn't going to accept that for a response," Jeffers added.

Harrison was in awe of what he was hearing. He was processing the information but struggling to link his father to the series of events. This was a story people only see in movies.

Jeffers went on, "Once this came out and the dust settled, the IRS offered him a handsome deal."

"Why did they offer him a deal?"

"They knew the rules governing Medicare reimbursement were confusing. They were embarrassed that someone like your dad was able to bill them and get away with it. They wanted their pound of flesh while they closed the insurance loopholes your father uncovered."

"And he refused?"

"Unfortunately. The deal required your dad to pay back $8 million, shut down the medical business, give up the few properties he owned at the time, and they would go away quietly."

"$8 million and all the other stuff doesn't sound like a minor penalty," Harrison responded.

"Considering your dad allegedly defrauded the United States for at least $15.5 million, trust me, Harrison, the deal was a bargain," Jeffers stated confidently.

"So, is that when he began to redirect his money into the real estate business?" Harrison inquired.

"Absolutely. He already had a few properties. However, he thought if he transferred dirty money from his medical business to the real estate business he would be able to keep it. That's when he started buying more apartment complexes around Indianapolis."

"So he was going to flee the country?" Harrison asked. He could barely comprehend everything he was hearing.

"Well, after the initial refusal, the special agent handling the matter became irate. They pulled the deal from the table and told him they were coming after him using every possible resource. In other words, they had every intention of sending him to prison for a very long time. Your father continued to fight using Jay Hausmann. In your father's defense, he thought he was still on the right side of the law. Why he thought that I don't know. This cat and mouse game went on for 18 months until your dad realized that he wasn't going to win."

Benton Jeffers paused. It was a lot to absorb.

"You ok?" Jeffers inquired.

Harrison found the story fascinating despite the fact it was his father. As disturbed as he was, he couldn't help but want to hear more. At this point, all Harrison could do was ask himself one question: why he didn't suspect this over the past 18 months?

"No, I'm not ok, but please continue," Harrison said encouragingly.

"Once your dad realized he was facing prison, the loss of his finances, his home, and his companies, he began to funnel money to the Cayman Islands. It appears he was planning to build a house. He purchased property, and he was transferring $5,000 to $10,000 at a time to the Cayman banks."

"Why the Caymans?" Harrison asked.

"The laws in the Cayman Islands are extremely lax. The government would have had no legal way of getting your dad back into the U.S., and the Cayman government wouldn't be obligated to cooperate."

Jeffers tried to simplify the details. Anything more would have been confusing.

"He had to know the government investigators were tracking him," Harrison presumed. "Wouldn't they keep close tabs on his bank accounts to see that money was moving in large sums?"

"This is where your father became sloppy. Keep in mind, Harrison, that people become desperate in times of stress. Your father, although very intelligent, was no different. He was fighting for survival. If your father had it his way, he and Victoria would be living in the Cayman Islands as of yesterday. The criminal agents figured it out when your dad purchased airline tickets. Now, here we sit."

Harrison didn't know how Benton Jeffers knew this information, but he wasn't about to ask. All of this information was not yet public. Harrison also knew Jeffers was doing him a favor by having this talk.

By legal rights, Jeffers shouldn't be having this discussion at all. Harrison wasn't well versed in law, but he knew enough to understand the attorney-client privilege.

"I only have one question," Harrison asked after a brief pause.

"What's Victoria's responsibility in this matter? She's an owner and a vice president of both companies, and she certainly was on her way to the Cayman Islands with my dad."

Jeffers chuckled ominously and shook his head. "She faces some charges, but she likely won't be arrested. She wasn't the one pulling the strings. She will likely get charged as an unindicted co-conspirator, which will bring her more shame than anything else. At this point, her fate depends on how much your father cooperates."

"What's left? They already have him."

"They have him. That much is true. Here's the real kicker. They believe your father has millions of dollars hidden elsewhere – money that is unrecovered. Where? I don't know. But they want to recover all the assets, and she is the pawn to encourage your dad to cooperate."

"So his cooperation is dependent upon how long he goes to prison?" Harrison asked.

Benton Jeffers nodded his head. "If they don't think your father is forthcoming with all his assets, they will seek the maximum sentence."

"What's the maximum sentence?"

"Between 15-to-20 years if he doesn't cooperate," Jeffers said as he kicked his feet up on his desk. "Five-to-seven years if he gives them everything they want. He'll probably be out two years early for good behavior in either case."

Harrison slumped in his chair and realized that even the best-case scenario was bad. It was devastating. He knew this would emotionally destroy Mimi.

Both men recognized there was nothing more to say. Slowly, they stood up and shook hands. Harrison thanked him for his time and asked to get in touch with him if he heard anything else that might be helpful.

"Take care, Harrison," Jeffers said somberly.

Harrison walked out and was reminded of a book his mother used to read to him as a child, *Alexander and the Terrible, Horrible, No Good, Very Bad Day*, by Judith Viorst.

"Ole' Alexander's got nothing on me."

SIXTEEN

"The righteous hate what is false,
but the wicked bring shame and disgrace."

HARRISON MARKS ARRIVED HOME STILL IN SHOCK FROM THE DAY'S events. On a typical weekday, he would return from work, finish a few emails, and call it a day. He would venture out to the back patio with a cold beer in hand to admire the tranquil lake. Today, the steel-blue water looked anything but tranquil.

If he stepped outside his home, he was convinced the neighbors in Hidden Shores would casually float their pontoon to his dock and ask about his father. If that didn't happen, he was wise enough to know that all eyes would be looking his way. Harrison knew his neighbors were discussing the event in detail and how they knew all along that Harlan Marks was going to end up in prison.

Staying inside was the best choice, at least for now. Besides, Harrison still had to contact Mimi, who had been calling him all day to find out when this misunderstanding would end. Harrison knew this was going to be a difficult phone call. He also knew he should go over to her apartment and have this discussion in person. Unfortunately for Mimi, he was exhausted.

Harrison had no idea how he was going to approach the conversation. He knew he wasn't going to tell her everything he learned today. He also avoided the fact that her son was reduced to tears on his exit from the courtroom a few short hours ago.

Mimi picked up the phone immediately in anticipation. Harrison suspected she was sitting by her phone all day. She had convinced herself that if she walked 15 feet into the kitchen, she wouldn't hear the ring, so Mimi stayed beside the phone all day. He smiled when he realized she likely hadn't been to the bathroom for the very same reason.

"Hello, Mimi," Harrison said without asking how she was doing.

"Oh, Harrison," she moaned. "I'm making myself sick thinking about this. Why haven't you called me?"

Harrison didn't feel like going through all the reasons he hadn't called. He had been gathering information all day to understand the story himself. Besides, he didn't want to talk to anybody but Claire. Regardless, he went through the day's events and only told her what she needed to know.

Harrison could hear his grandmother choking back tears as he talked. While Harrison and his grandmother were very close, nothing could get in the way of her love for her son. Not even Harrison. He knew he had to choose every word carefully. Further, he wasn't about to throw his grandmother's son under the bus. The newspapers and other media outlets were doing a great job on their own.

"Is it true what's being said about him?" she whimpered.

"I'm afraid a lot was going on with Dad that we didn't realize. It will take a long time to sort everything out. We need to get used to the idea that he'll be in the downtown jail for some time."

Harrison didn't want to answer the next question, but he knew it was coming.

"How long?"

"At least a couple of months until the attorneys work this out."

He knew it was going to be longer, but no sense in overwhelming her.

Harrison went on to share that her son had an opportunity to settle the issue and keep himself out of prison many months ago. He didn't think it registered with the old lady. Right now, she just wanted to be comforted.

"Oh, Harrison, I just wish I were dead."

At that time, Claire walked through the door. Harrison never heard the garage door open but was so relieved to see her. She tried to smile but it was not the natural smile that he was accustomed to seeing. He didn't care. She was home, and they could talk, or at least regroup. Unfortunately, he still had to deal with his grandmother who wanted her life to end.

"I will look into visiting hours so we can see him." He didn't want to talk about her last comment, and he wanted to provide her with a little hope and something to look forward to.

Harrison hung up the phone.

Claire leaned against the kitchen counter while Harrison stood in the middle of the living room with not a single word spoken. Sadness overcame them as Harrison walked over to embrace his wife.

"This isn't about us," he said, trying to remind his wife of all the good things to come. He rubbed her stomach and tried to get her to smile.

Claire nodded and gave a slight grin with a tear running down her face. Harrison could tell the day was stressful.

"People wanted to know, Harrison. They never said anything, but they kept coming to my office and asking if I was ok."

Claire was always a very private person. She only portrayed happy moments in front of her co-workers.

"I'm sorry, Claire. I'm so sorry. I wish this could be different."

Harrison hugged his pregnant wife tightly. He was struggling too, but he had to show strength for his family. Harrison was a grown man, and grown men needed to comfort themselves.

Phone conversations with his mom, Claire's parents, and again with Mimi consumed the entire evening. Soon it was time for bed, and they knew their anxiety would grow as they faced another new day.

Harrison lay silent in bed, but his mind wouldn't let him rest. It was impossible to reconcile the situation although he tried desperately.

His father became someone he didn't know. Even after watching him go through two divorces and come into money, Harrison felt he knew the real Harlan Marks. Harrison knew his father was a shrewd man, but he never thought he was a man that crossed the line of ethical wrongdoing. Harlan's actions were deceitful.

It was hard for Harrison to comprehend. Every child learns that lying is unacceptable. Those that did lie must suffer the consequences. His dad instilled fear into Harrison that the lie better be good because if he found out, the consequences would be horrific.

It happened one time, and Harrison learned his lesson for good. Being deceitful was a bad option.

Harrison remembered when he was nine years old, and his mother made him a hot dog and baked beans for dinner. Well, his mother poured baked beans out of a can and didn't bother to add seasoning. As a result, the beans were bland and inedible, which wasn't unusual for his mother, who always struggled in the kitchen.

Harrison voiced his displeasure, but his father told him he had to sit at the table until his baked beans were gone.

His parents retired to the living room for the evening while Harrison sat at the table to finish the beans. It was then that he hatched a brilliant plan.

The family dog was a female Doberman named Dixie. She wandered into the kitchen, where Harrison remained sitting in the dark.

I'll give them to the dog, he thought wisely.

He held the bowl of tasteless baked beans in the air for Dixie to eat. Harrison was smart enough not to place the bowl on the floor. The dog would have shoved the bowl across the tile making enough noise to get them both in trouble.

Dixie licked the beans over and over but pulled away. The dog wouldn't eat the beans either.

Harrison placed the bowl back on the table right before his father walked into the kitchen.

"Finish the damn meal!" he yelled.

Harrison looked at the beans that not only tasted horrible but had now been licked by the dog. He couldn't tell his father what happened. He had to sit and eat the beans while cursing his dad and Dixie the entire time.

"Yes, deceit is bad. It always catches up to you," he stated.

Harrison found himself slowly waking up and knew he hadn't had a good night's sleep. He got up and shuffled to his phone to make an early morning call to the Marion County Jail.

After a frustrating conversation with a lady that didn't like her job, Harrison found that visiting hours were only on Sunday at 9 a.m., which wasn't horrible except they only allowed 12 visitors, and it was first come, first serve. The voice on the other end of the phone recommended that he arrive no later than 7:30 a.m. to secure his visit as people are sent home once the list is full.

To get there on time, Harrison needed to pick up his grandmother no later than 7 a.m., which meant he needed to leave home no later than 6:45 a.m., which meant he needed to be up on Sunday morning no later than 6:15 a.m..

The morning was not going to be easy.

However, Harrison felt it was his responsibility to help Mimi see her son. It also allowed him to ask questions and get his father's perspective. Could it be this was just a misunderstanding? Maybe there was a simple explanation?

Harrison picked up his grandmother precisely at 7 a.m. He suspected that Mimi never went to bed in anticipation of seeing her son.

The streets of Indianapolis were empty. They walked into the Marion County Jail and were asked to remove belts, jewelry, and everything from their pockets. They both had to take off their shoes and place them on the belt before signing in. Harrison felt he was going through security at the Indianapolis International Airport but this was worse.

The two signed in and waited for an hour. After a quick observation, Harrison determined the unhappy lady on the phone was correct about the arrival time. He and his grandmother signed in as visitor numbers eight and nine. The other individuals who arrived only 15 minutes later were shut out and sent home.

After playing a few games on his cell phone and Mimi sitting still and staring straight ahead, they were called to the elevator. All cell phones had to be given to the security guard.

A very smelly elevator ride and 20 seconds later they all arrived at the 4th floor.

"Please remain inside the elevator once the doors open. We will advise you when to proceed to your assigned table," the guard in the elevator advised.

Harrison should have known to repeat the message to his 90-year-old grandmother who was hard of hearing. Once the doors opened, she made a quick attempt toward Harlan. The guard quickly nabbed her.

"I said remain inside the elevator, Ma'am. Is it that difficult to understand?"

"She has a difficult time hearing. You don't need to scold her," Harrison declared to the guard.

"If you want to see your inmate, then you will abide by my authority and the jailhouse rules," said the guard, as he squared himself looking directly into Harrison's eyes.

"Do you understand?"

"Yes," replied Harrison completely irritated.

The prisoners were assigned a table, and then visitors were allowed to proceed. The final instruction was to sit opposite the prisoner and not on the same side. This prevented any capers or funny business that might take place.

Harrison made sure to guide his grandmother to her seat, despite trying to sit next to Harlan and break the rules again. One more mischievous outburst from the 90-year-old, 85-pound lady could earn her a free night in the stockade next to her son.

Harlan looked terrible. Harrison had never seen his father look so defeated and weak. Despite sporting his prison assigned brown jumpsuit and cardboard slippers, Harlan tried to be strong, but Harrison knew it was a show for him, but especially for his mother. He knew she couldn't bear to see him sad, let alone cry. Although that's what it looked like Harlan had been doing for the past five days.

Mimi didn't have anything to say. She also didn't have anything to ask. It was as if she was content just being there – she didn't need to know and was convinced this was a big mistake. She was convinced her son was innocent. In her eyes, he was a wonderful son, an outstanding husband and father, and that was all that mattered. According to her, they should let him go on those traits alone. All she wanted to do was be with him.

After realizing his grandmother had very little to say and knowing the time limit, Harrison began his line of questioning.

"What the hell happened?"

Harlan chuckled at his son's forthcoming.

"I didn't do it," Harlan quipped. "All of us in here are innocent."

It was another lousy attempt at humor, which didn't even crack a smile on Harrison's face.

He sat silent, staring directly at his father, waiting for a proper response.

"I'm serious, to an extent," his father rebuffed. "All the things I did with the business were above water according to the laws. They're just looking to make me a scapegoat."

"A scapegoat? For what?" Harrison asked in disbelief.

"Are you kidding? Look how much money I was able to make from Medicare over the past few years. Do you think they want that to get out? Do you think they want other people doing what I'm doing and finding ways to make a good living because the federal government has no idea what it's doing? They don't understand their own rules. I do know what the rules state, Harrison. I have scoured their laws, and I know them better than anyone. Now they feel threatened. They have to take me down to scare others from pursuing the same method of business."

"Same method of business? Do you mean fraud?" Harrison said, trying to keep it under his breath.

"Oh, stop with your righteousness, Harrison. I've done nothing wrong according to the letter of the law."

Harrison didn't know enough about the laws of Medicare to battle his father on this subject. He moved to another topic.

"I understand they offered you a deal a long time ago that could have kept you out of this place," Harrison stated as he looked around the sterile and lifeless room.

"I suppose they did," Harlan said in a surprised way. *How did his son know all the details*, he thought.

"It wasn't a deal. I turn over everything I own and sleep on the street in exchange for staying out of prison."

"So what's next?" Harrison asked. Mimi's ears perked up, and she re-engaged in the conversation.

"I'm still hopeful Hausmann can get me a deal. I don't want to take this to trial. If I lose, I'll go away for a long time. That's not a chance I'm willing to take. I'm hoping for the best, but I'm not very good at this waiting game."

Harrison knew that all too well.

"But I'm doing alright," Harlan added as if someone had asked the question. "The other inmates see me as a big shot. They refer to me as The Whale. I get respect."

Harrison's eyebrows furled. He had no desire to hear what the others thought of his father. It was yet another example of his father prioritizing status over family.

At that moment, Harrison began to question the purpose of both. He suffered through his parents' marriage, listening to them argue every day over things that didn't matter. In the final year of their marriage, his mother never came home until after Harrison went to bed. Because he was an only child, Harrison was forced to deal with their dysfunction on his own. Harrison listened to the verbal daggers, but he had no option but to ride the storm. Fortunately, they lived in the country, and the closest neighbors were hundreds of yards away.

When he was 15, he found out his mother was no longer committed to the relationship. She wanted out and had found someone else. The other person explained why she was never home until after Harrison was in bed. He only saw his mother in the mornings before school and on weekends. Harrison never understood why he didn't pick up on her whereabouts before.

While his mother remarried successfully, his father had a broken heart that never healed. Harrison knew his father was no saint, but he also believed no one deserved this fate.

As a result, Harlan married a second time when Harrison was 16. He married a woman who was both verbally and physically abusive. The world doesn't hear much about abusive women, but he and his father discovered firsthand that they exist. Thrown dishware and empty wine bottles disfigured the walls in the Brownsburg, Indiana house that appeared family centered from the outside but was the devil's playground behind closed doors. Coincidentally, her previous husband committed suicide.

Eighteen months later, wife number two did the Marks' men a favor by pulling a knife on Harlan over a minor disagreement. Harlan spent the rest of the evening in a local hotel while Harrison went to stay with his mother.

The next afternoon, Harlan went back to the house only to find all of his belongings piled on the driveway. She poured gasoline over his clothes but was kind enough not to set them on fire.

Harrison received a call after school from his father, "Harrison, you need to come home and gather your belongings. We need to move out. Things have escalated, and it's no longer safe to live here."

Harrison skipped baseball practice and arrived home to find two police cars in front of his house and every neighbor staring from their front yards.

Father and son moved to an apartment until Harrison's second year at Butler University. At that time, Harrison decided to find a roommate and live in an apartment closer to campus.

It was then, Harlan met Victoria.

Harrison found himself reflecting on his family life that failed him for so long. It was a life that brought happy times, but also littered with disappointment and confusion.

If childhood is supposed to be the easy years, then what does it mean for an adult? If history is any indication of the future, what were the chances to become a good husband and father?

Now a young adult, married and about to have a child of his own, he was again on shaky ground through no fault of his own.

Was this the journey intended for him? Emotionally this was gut-wrenching enough. Spiritually, however, this couldn't be what his higher power intended, but here he was facing life-crushing blows. Something, or someone, was allowing these events to take place. Was it God who was allowing Harrison to be a target even after He had given his life to Christ as a 20-year-old young man during his second year in college?

It was true. Spring break took place over Easter, and Harrison used the week to visit an elementary school friend who moved to Birmingham, AL. Alan and his family were deeply rooted in their faith, which Harrison always admired.

Alan and Harrison traveled to Orlando to meet a few of Alan's fraternity brothers. They all attended church on Easter Sunday. Harrison found peace that week being around others who were born again Christians.

At the end of the sermon, the pastor asked the congregation to bow their heads. As the pastor began to pray, he asked members of the congregation who haven't yet committed themselves to a life with Jesus Christ to look up at him.

Harrison looked directly at the pastor, and he acknowledged his gaze. Harrison felt redeemed.

He was brought back to reality when a booming voice came over the speaker. "Wrap it up", the guard stated.

Visitors and inmates were allowed one last hug goodbye. Mimi happily took the opportunity to hold tight to her son and tell him she would see him next week. Harrison wasn't certain.

Harlan showed his bravery as he watched his mother and son walk onto the elevator. The doors slowly closed with everyone waving and blowing kisses to their family or friend – well, everyone except Harrison.

SEVENTEEN

"Discretion will protect you,
and understanding will guard you."

Sunday visits to the downtown jail went on for five weeks. With each passing week, Harrison and his grandmother became familiar with the cumbersome prison rules and processes. They were now offering advice to other visitors who were being hounded by the boorish guards. The two also synchronized themselves perfectly to arrive at the parking garage in time to be the last to sign in and ensure the least amount of time in the waiting area.

It all became a means to an end. Harrison began to apply the same rule of engagement at home. He was always one to map out his workday, but now he found himself doing the same for his alone time. Mow the lawn, wash the cars, pay the bills, finish the evening with office emails and plan for the next day. It was all part of the process to pass the time. The more Harrison planned his day, the more he could avoid thinking about his father.

Claire wasn't getting the best of Harrison during this time, but she was always self-sufficient. When she arrived home from work, Harrison had pizza on order or his famous "yellow dinner" – grilled cheese, corn, and chicken noodle soup from a can. All things yellow. It wasn't a loving attempt to make things easier for his wife as much as it required less thought for both. Harrison was becoming more about the process and less about the people who loved him.

Claire worked hard to be understanding. She knew the demands Mimi put on her husband to make sure she was taxied each Sunday to downtown

Indianapolis. Claire also knew that Harrison carried the emotional burden of listening to her cry on the phone precisely at 8:30 each night.

It didn't help that Harrison was an only child. He had no one else to share the hardship. He had to do everything.

As a child, he resented his mother and father for having only one child. He felt robbed of the companionship of a brother or sister. Now it would be a luxury. He needed a sibling to help him through the emotional burden. But having a sibling was not meant to be, given that his parents lost what would have been an older brother two years before Harrison came along.

Due to an inoperable heart defect, Baby-Boy Marks died three days after birth. Harrison remembered April 6th, as this was the first day that his parents took him to the cemetery and had a picnic next to the tombstone. Harrison was eight years old when he inquired what the trip was all about. The tragic loss led to his adoption one year later.

But none of that mattered now. Harrison could only deal with what was happening at the moment.

While he struggled with his battles, Claire battled internally. She was slowly becoming resentful that she wasn't able to celebrate her pregnancy like other expectant mothers. Shopping for a crib, clothes, and other baby accessories became a list of things to do, rather than an opportunity to bond with her husband and look forward to days to come.

Harrison assumed she was content. He assumed he was checking things off his list that was making it easier for her and, at the same time, easier on him. The communication between the two was becoming strained. Her husband was so focused on solving problems that he failed to focus on his wife. He became the problem.

The challenge became even more difficult on the second Wednesday in October when the house phone rang.

"May I please speak with Mr. or Mrs. Marks?" asked the unidentified voice on the other end.

"This is Mr. Marks."

"Mr. Marks, this is Special Agent Andrew Spawn with the Criminal Division of the Internal Revenue Service. I am responsible for handling the continuing investigation regarding the Harlan Marks matter. Mr. Marks, can I verify that Harlan Marks is your father?"

"Yes, he is. What is this about?"

"Sir, through our investigation of Mr. Mark's and his assets we found that you and your wife have purchased a house in which Mr. Marks held the banknote. Given this situation, the asset has been seized and is now the property of the United States Government until the matter is resolved. We need to schedule a time to come to the property and take a video of the inside and outside. We must ensure the structure remains intact throughout the investigation."

Harrison could not believe what he was hearing. He felt his body temperature increase starting in his feet and traveling quickly to his head.

"Hello? Hello?" repeated the voice on the other end of the phone.

Harrison knew he had to say something. Mustering all he could to be partially intelligent he responded, "I'll be contacting my attorney."

Harrison hung up the phone without saying another word. A terrible situation just got worse. He felt paralyzed. Harrison began to shake, and he fell backward onto the bed. He never made a sound, but his head was exploding with emotion. He labored to breathe.

I'm losing my house, he thought. *Everything I have worked and saved for is gone! This can't be happening. How am I going to tell Claire?*

Harrison and Claire were always indirectly affected, but now they were a part of the storyline.

Did I just tell that guy I was going to contact my attorney? I don't even have an attorney, he thought.

Until now, Harrison was able to suppress himself. It was hard, but he could at least remain optimistic. He became terrified for the first time in his life. The outcome, which now directly affected him, was beyond his control.

Before Harrison knew it, an hour had passed. It was nearly 5 p.m., and Claire would be home soon.

He gathered his thoughts and called his stepfather. Fred was a tremendous friend to Harrison. In many ways, Fred filled the fatherly role of support and love that his father had trouble providing.

His stepfather was a bank vice-president responsible for the commercial loans department. He was nearing retirement age, and through the years, had gained the trust of many businesses in the Indianapolis community. He developed contacts who were small business owners or high-level executives for larger corporations. He was a good man who loved Harrison's mother very much.

Fred had two children from his previous marriage and was still able to treat his stepson as one of his own. Harrison could not ask for a better stepfather.

Each time Harrison and Claire went to dinner with his mom and stepdad, Fred saw people he knew. More importantly, people seemed to know him. He had a celebrity-like status amongst the business community, so it seemed.

His stepfather's business relationships would turn out to be an advantage for Harrison and Claire. A person who had connections would be able to suggest an attorney worthy of protecting the younger Marks' financial interest.

"Fred, I'm sorry to call you at work and I need your help."

"Hey, Harrison. Are you ok?"

"Listen. I have a problem, and I need your help," Harrison repeated while trying to mask the fear in his voice.

It wasn't working. Fred knew Harrison was troubled. "I'll do what I can. What's wrong?"

"I just received a call from a special agent with the IRS. They seized our house because of my dad's arrest. They want me to sign an agreement and they want to take a video of the home. Are they allowed to do this? Is this within their right?"

"Oh, my," Fred said calmly. "I was afraid this could happen."

The comment surprised Harrison but also gave him comfort. Fred seemed prepared for a situation his stepson wasn't considering. He was glad this didn't catch everyone off guard. He now had someone who could share his perspective.

Fred paused a moment and explained. "Harrison, the original loan was directly tied to your dad since you purchased the house from him and not from a bank."

"Therefore, it probably is within their right," Fred continued. "They seized the house believing your dad is still the rightful owner. It's the same way any financial lender owns a house until the final mortgage payment is made."

"But I have a contract that involved an attorney. The purchase was done legally, and we even refinanced," Harrison exclaimed as if he had to convince his stepdad.

"I know, I know. I'm not saying you shouldn't fight. I'm just saying the federal government is looking to seize every asset that could be tied to your dad. This is the way they recoup their losses. This is unfortunately how they also apply pressure to get what they want."

"I need an attorney; that's why I called," Harrison mentioned.

"Agreed. I want you to call Molly Eckles. She is a partner with Kane & Eckles Law Firm in Carmel, Indiana. I helped get their firm started 10 years ago, and I hear good things about her. She is an excellent defense attorney."

Harrison wrote the name down and thanked him.

"I suggest you give her a call right away," encouraged Fred. "You need to act fast as the government can tighten the noose pretty quickly."

That last comment didn't comfort Harrison much, but he also knew it was true.

"Have you shared this with Claire?"

"Not yet," Harrison responded somberly. "I wanted to have a plan in place before she gets home. You've at least given me a start, so thank you."

"You're welcome, Harrison. I'll let your mom know what's going on, but please keep us informed if you don't mind. I love you."

"Thank you. I love you too."

Harrison hung up the phone and immediately searched for the number. It didn't take long before the receptionist answered. Harrison left a message and begged the receptionist to make sure Molly Eckles called him back as soon as possible.

Until now, he was angry with his father and with the IRS, but he never placed blame. He felt his father was at fault, and Harlan needed to pay for the crime. That was fair and realistic. But Harlan also realized the government's arrogant approach to make an example out of the older Marks.

Now Harrison was being dragged down. He was no longer a spectator watching from the sidelines. He was directly involved, and now his concern for his father's well-being had diminished. Harrison had to focus on himself, his wife, and their unborn child.

For the first time in months, he went to the liquor cabinet and poured himself a drink. He felt cornered and accused. Someone needed to be blamed. It may be his father, or it may be the government. Maybe God could have helped somewhere along the way. According to him, all three could have handled the situation differently.

Where is this coming from? I don't deserve this, he thought silently.

Harrison assumed he did enough to turn his spiritual life around. He seemed to think God had a presence in his life when he committed himself to Christ eight years ago. The spiritual intervention experienced during that spring break created a deeper relationship, or so he thought.

Harrison was trying so hard to listen to God's voice, but he must have misinterpreted the message. Maybe he didn't have an open line of communication with God after all. Maybe God wasn't even on his side.

How could He be on his side and still allow this to happen? Harrison felt like an outsider. He couldn't gain traction with God. How does that happen? Was he that much of an outsider that he couldn't connect with The One who supposedly wants a relationship with everyone?

Harrison understood tests of faith, but he wondered how far this had to go. He felt isolated. He thought he picked himself up, but only to stumble and fall a second time. Harrison questioned if it was God who was grabbing him by the ankles. He thought God may consider doing this to thieves, drug dealers, or murderers, but someone like him who didn't have any control over the outcome was cruel.

Regardless, with his house seized, he was under government control and felt his spirit breaking. He knew the IRS needed access to his savings and checking accounts, investments, and other belongings.

He wanted God to throw him a life vest. Instead, He threw him a weighted vest, and he was sinking.

The phone rang, and Harrison was startled. It was the law office of Kane and Eckles.

Harrison answered quickly. After a formal greeting, he told Molly Eckles his relationship with Fred. She perked up once his name was mentioned.

"I have a tremendous amount of respect for your stepfather," Molly added.

Eckles waited for Harrison to continue.

"You have likely heard the case related to Harlan Marks and his recent arrest for defrauding Medicare," Harrison added.

"I'm familiar with it," she stated with anticipation to learn more.

"Well, I'm Harlan Marks' son."

Harrison knew a response was coming, and he was right.

"Oh," a long pause ensued.

Harrison knew the entire Indianapolis community was talking about the man that defrauded millions of dollars from the government but he was secretly hoping to explain the case to someone who hadn't heard anything about the matter.

"I know he's in trouble, but please fill me in on the details," Molly stated.

"He's in a lot of trouble, Molly, and I thought that was enough stress in my life until today. I just received a phone call from a man named Andrew Spawn who claimed he's a special agent for the Criminal Division of the Internal Revenue Service."

Harrison's stress level increased. He shared the recent phone call and how the case now involved him, his family, and his home.

Harrison could only envision the look on Molly Eckles' face as he recalled the story in full detail. If he were in her shoes, he would have been motioning for every attorney in the firm to come into the room as he placed the client on speakerphone. It was a story too good to keep to yourself.

Eckles, in contrast, listened intently. On more than one occasion, she asked him to slow down while she took notes and asked for more details. Harrison complied.

"Ok, please keep going, Harrison," Eckles encouraged. "Tell me about the house and the purchase contract with your dad."

With as much detail as possible, Harrison described the contract. After 30 minutes, Eckles felt she had enough information to do some research.

Harrison felt vindicated. He won nothing at this point other than gaining an advocate willing to fight on his behalf. It was a step in the right direction for Harrison when he needed it the most.

As a communication major in college, and now a salesperson for a Fortune 500 company, he was well-versed at reading people, even if it was over the phone. He liked Molly Eckles.

"Can you and your wife come on Saturday morning? I want time to think about this and get input from other attorneys. We need to discuss this further and weigh the options. But please know, before you leave here on Saturday, we will have a strategy. How does that sound?"

Molly Eckles presented herself as professional, energetic, and highly capable. Fred had come through for his stepson once again. Hope no longer seemed elusive.

But Harrison still had a hurdle to cross. He had to share the bad news with Claire and somehow find a way to make it sound like he had it under control. Worse yet, he had to convince her that everything was going to be alright, even if he wasn't sure it was true.

He heard the car door shut, and seconds later, Claire walked into the house.

EIGHTEEN

"Listen to advise and accept instruction,
that you may gain wisdom in the future."

CLAIRE CRIED WHEN SHE HEARD THE NEWS. HER RESPONSE WAS NOT unexpected. Given the circumstances, Harrison knew anyone would have done the same. However, he did notice that Claire had been crying a lot lately.

She was seven months pregnant, and her emotions were high. It was hard to see the line between pregnancy and stress.

What he did know, however, was that his wife didn't need outside influences impacting her emotional state. Unfortunately, this fight couldn't be avoided.

She took the news hard, but now the circumstances were different. The fight came to her doorstep with the threat of taking her house. Everything she and Harrison worked so hard to achieve was now in jeopardy. Claire's frustration was warranted because she knew that she and Harrison had done everything the right way. Their approach to earning money and raising a family was a carefully planned roadmap.

"What are you thinking?" Harrison asked apprehensively.

Claire couldn't even look at Harrison. Her eyes were filled with tears. His wife didn't need to speak to show her overwhelming grief, and it didn't require an expert at non-verbal cues to notice. He saw the pain on Claire's face and tears falling on her lap. He knew what she was thinking.

Harrison was already sitting next to her on the couch. He moved even closer and put his arm around her to pull her closer.

"Our appointment with the attorney is tomorrow. Fred highly recommended her, and when I spoke with her on the phone, she sounded capable," Harrison mentioned again.

He shared the information with Claire earlier, although he knew she needed to hear the positive news at least one more time.

It was a sleepless night for both, and neither one spoke. Their minds raced as each played out different outcomes from best to worst.

The morning didn't come soon enough. The Marks arrived 30 minutes early for their appointment.

At precisely 10 a.m., a beautiful strawberry blonde who was 12 years their elder walked into the lobby to greet the young couple. Eckles was confident, and it showed in her stride. She was as fit as she was tall. The trendy lawyer stood 5'10" and weighed 140 pounds, according to Harrison's thorough evaluation. She dressed casually, yet professionally, for her Saturday morning meeting.

When Claire noticed her husband was slightly enamored, she provided an elbow to his ribs as they followed her to the conference room. He pretended to be surprised by his wife's response, but Claire was also well-skilled when it came to the non-verbal world.

A person can not, not communicate, they learned from their communication days at Butler.

She led them to a conference room where she organized stacks of paper placed in separate piles. Molly Eckles had done her homework. Within 24 hours, she educated herself on the entire case – well beyond what the newspapers and television reported.

She knew details of the police chase. Eckles also had more information about Harlan and Victoria's properties and holdings in the Cayman Islands.

"How do you know these things?" he asked. "You haven't been involved to the level that I am, and some of what you are saying is news to me."

"Well, I'm involved now. It's my job to know things," Eckles smiled confidently as if she had everything under control.

Harrison and Claire looked skeptically at Eckles, who appeared to be taunting them with her background on the case.

She lit up for a moment to share what she was holding back.

"I know your father's attorney very well. I worked for Jay Hausmann while I was putting myself through law school. I gave him a call early this morning and he was gracious enough to share details that may not otherwise be shared between counselors."

She went on. "However, you need to understand that Hausmann is furious that the IRS brought you into this mudslinging. He wants you to be able to keep the house because you deserve it. From what I have learned, you purchased the property within the rights of the law. That's what we need to talk about today. How do we protect you and your assets?"

Harrison was impressed. More importantly, Claire was impressed. The couple felt like someone had their best interest in mind and could do something about it.

Maybe this isn't going to be such a long process after all, Harrison thought.

After a quick sip of coffee, Eckles continued, "You need to realize this could be a long process. These things can take time, especially with a high-profile case."

Harrison was focused on getting this matter resolved. Claire, on the other hand, wanted to know why she and her husband were involved.

"You mentioned the IRS and mudslinging, Molly. Why are they seizing our house and involving us if everybody knows we purchased the house legally? We've done nothing wrong, right?" Claire inquired.

"Great question, Claire. This recent action against you tells me one thing. Your father-in-law is not cooperating with the government. It's not uncommon for them to apply pressure on family members. The government tries to hurt the family financially when criminal acts like this take place. They will leave no stone unturned."

"Also know," Eckles looked directly at Harrison, "your father embarrassed the federal government. He found a way to scam money right under their nose. Even after they found out about it, they couldn't do anything to stop him because they didn't have enough evidence. He continued to take their money and that pissed them off more than you know. If I understand one thing about the IRS, it's that you don't make a fool out of them while taking their money in the process. They are going to make an example of your father, so others don't try to do the same."

Harrison and Claire thought for a moment. It made sense.

"You mentioned that my father wasn't cooperating. What do you know, and why wouldn't he cooperate?" Harrison asked.

Eckles was waiting for this question. "When I spoke with Hausmann, he said that your father has been defiant ever since the IRS approached him and told him to cease and desist. In other words, Harrison, your dad sounds like a real asshole who thinks he's above the law."

Claire rolled her eyes as if she knew exactly what Eckles meant. The attorney was clearly talking about the same Harlan Marks.

Eckles continued, "Things have not improved since he turned himself over to authorities. Hausmann has tried to encourage your father to cooperate, but he thinks he knows better than his attorney. Furthermore, he doesn't think he's done anything wrong. Now, the IRS and U.S. Assistant Attorney aren't wasting time. If they can't get him to work with them, then they will put pressure on the people he loves until he cooperates."

Harrison's face turned red. The two women in the room could see that he was furious with his father. Harrison knew that his father only had his interest in mind.

Eckles continued. "With the amount of money your father reportedly stole from Medicare, they are going to use every means necessary to get back as much money as possible to avoid further embarrassment."

"Our portion is a drop in the bucket compared to the millions he stole. Even if we paid them every bit of what this house is worth, it still wouldn't make a dent in the overall amount," Harrison pleaded.

"Did you hear me say that your father wasn't cooperating?" Eckles stated sarcastically.

She was sharp and capable, but her bedside manner needed some work.

"There's one more thing," Eckles implied. "Your step-mom, what's her name?"

"Victoria", both Marks stated disgustedly at the same time.

"The federal government is applying pressure to her as well. They have already charged her as an unindicted co-conspirator. From my understanding, they are threatening to charge her as a co-conspirator if your father doesn't cooperate," Eckles stated.

"Trust me," she continued. "These people are first-class pricks. We don't want to give into them, but we don't want to act like your father either."

"We are innocent bystanders in this whole mess," Harrison mentioned. "If we are guilty of anything, we're guilty of being naïve."

Molly finally offered a genuine smile. "I couldn't agree more."

She gave Harrison and Claire a moment of silence to collect themselves.

"So are we going to do this?" Eckles asked with a spark of enthusiasm.

Claire chimed in, "I thought we already were."

"Great. I'm going to make this easy for you. We are not going to sign the Property Forfeiture Agreement. We will likely lose this battle in the long run, but we don't want to roll over. Regardless, we're going to make the government work for it. Plus, this will buy me time to contact David Costello, the

U.S. Assistant Attorney. I want to see how serious they are about you two. We'll figure out what he wants and use that as our starting point."

"If my father starts to cooperate, is it a possibility they may leave us alone?" Harrison asked.

"I hope so. It's a strong possibility, that's for sure," Eckles was cautious with the next response. "Even if your father starts to cooperate, he may have already pissed them off too much to turn back. Your old man's a real gem."

Claire then raised a question to which she already had the answer. "Could our involvement have been avoided if he would have cooperated from the start?"

Eckles's answer stung more than Claire could have anticipated. "The incident could have been avoided from the time Harlan was first approached. It could have been avoided well after he hired Jay Hausmann, and it could have been avoided at the time he turned himself over."

Harrison and Claire sunk in their seats.

Molly Eckles advised her new clients she would be in touch as they shook hands and walked out of the lobby and back to their car.

"Are you hungry?" Harrison asked.

The one-hour consultation lasted nearly two hours.

"No," she answered without looking up.

"I hate that man," Claire whispered while choking back tears.

The 10-minute ride home was going to be a silent one.

NINETEEN

"A fool shows his annoyance at once,
but a prudent man overlooks an insult."

For A LONG TIME, HARRISON AND CLAIRE WENT THROUGH THE motions. Their daily routine consisted of work, eating leftovers, then settling in for the night. The routine was expected and comfortable for the young couple who didn't have a social calendar, especially during the workweek.

To be clear, they never cared for having their weeks filled with social gatherings, and they weren't about to change now. Now was a time to remain low and out of the spotlight. It was the best way to avoid questions they didn't care to answer.

Harrison tried to convince Claire they should go for a walk or maybe even a boat ride to watch the sunset across the lake. Claire often agreed, but tonight she was tired with a lot on her mind. Harrison understood.

Their second favorite place to gather was the bedroom shortly after dinner. Not for romantic reasons, but because it was comfortable for Claire. She wanted to lay down with her feet up. Around 7 p.m., Harrison would recline on the king-size bed and turn on the television. He and Claire didn't care for shows, but it did provide some much-needed background noise while they scrolled through social media. Harrison enjoyed the political takes, sports updates, and the many pictures provided by his high school and college friends. Claire was much different. She loved posting on social media, and her friends could expect at least one picture per day of the rowdy dog.

The pug came into the room next. Zoe launched herself onto the bed once she realized Harrison was daring her to join him. The bed sat high off the ground and occasionally Zoe would mis-time the jump and crash into the side of the mattress. Most of the time, however, if she had a running start from the hallway, she nailed the landing.

Claire was always last, but never too far behind. It was a relief for Harrison to see his favorite girl walk through the door as it was the one room he never liked to be alone. He enjoyed listening to her talk and tell him about her day while he sat silent and nodded a few times to let her know he was listening. It was comforting to him, although many times Claire felt she was talking to the wall.

This night was no different.

Harrison's cell phone rang at 9:30 p.m.

"Uh oh," he stated to Claire.

Occasionally, a customer would call with a delivery issue scheduled for the evening. Most of his customers worked three shifts, and they needed deliveries to sustain production. Those calls usually meant a late evening for Harrison. He had to contact the production team to determine when the truck should hit the road to show up at his customer's dock.

However, an unrecognizable number appeared on his phone. He thought it was another solicitation call wanting to sell him an extended warranty on his car or offer him a consolidation deal for outstanding debt on his credit cards. They were all scam artists hoping to take advantage of an unsuspecting person, and Harrison wasn't going to have it. Regardless, it seemed late even for solicitors to call. He took the call, expecting to play along with the scammer on the other end.

"Mr. Marks, this is Andrew Spawn, Special Agent for The Internal Revenue Service."

Harrison didn't need Spawn to give his full-scale credentials. He already recognized the name and hated him. It had to be Spawn empowering himself while attempting to intimidate others. It worked. Spawn suffered from small-man syndrome, but he had a deep voice that commanded a room.

Harrison put that aside. He was shocked to hear his voice. He was more concerned since Molly Eckles called David Costello three weeks earlier to advise the government authorities that all questions or requests for the Marks would now be directed to her. Just yesterday the younger Marks lost their court petition to release the lien on the home and were forced to sign the forfeiture agreement.

"You know you're supposed to be contacting my attorney Molly Eckles?" Harrison continued, "Calling me is not only out of protocol, but it is extremely unprofessional."

He surprised himself with his bravado and willingness to stand his ground, but with his back against the wall, he felt he didn't have anything to lose.

Spawn was not to be outdone and dug in.

"Listen, I've got a search warrant for your home right here in my hands that says I can come to your house right now and turn the place upside down if I so desire. Now, I don't want to do that. But, if you want to act defiantly, I'm happy to make that happen. Since we seized the property, I want to come by tomorrow and take a video of the house on the inside and outside. I thought you and I could set a time rather than involve the attorneys. Regardless, I'm coming tomorrow."

Harrison was stunned. He recalled that Spawn mentioned coming to the house during his initial phone call a week ago. It was overlooked when Spawn advised him that the house had been seized.

When the couple sat down with Molly a day earlier to sign the agreement, she told them the video needed to happen. Harrison and Claire came to terms with letting them into the house; they just expected it to happen more politely and through their attorney. Unfortunately, that's not how Spawn worked.

Harrison backed down from the fight knowing this was not a battle he could win. Molly advised him of the overall goal – get the house back since the Marks felt it was rightfully theirs. Cooperation was the best step in that direction.

Claire remained silent and picked up the conversation from both ends.

"OK," Harrison relented. "I still want to talk to Molly in the morning to get her input."

"Call her if you like, but somebody needs to call me with a time. Otherwise, I'll show up when it's most convenient for me and let myself in – if you know what I mean," Spawn added just before hanging up.

With the phone still in his hand, Harrison turned in disbelief to Claire. She couldn't offer any reassurance. Harrison felt his body go numb while his heart began to race. It was a feeling he recognized all too well in the past few weeks.

He immediately texted Molly, expecting her to respond. It didn't happen. The conversation needed to wait until the morning. It was another sleepless night for the soon-to-be parents.

Eckles received a call from Harrison precisely at 8 a.m. She saw the text the night before. It infuriated her that Spawn dared to contact her client after she informed Costello that she was the point of contact. It was by code and ethics that any form of communication should be from the two representing attorneys.

Further, it wasn't that she didn't want to respond to her client the night before. It related more to her state of mind. She knew that a phone call from Spawn directly to the Marks and a few adult drinks would not produce a professional conversation.

"Good morning, Harrison," Eckles answered the phone. "I think I know why you're calling."

"Molly, they want to come today to take a video of the house. What is going on, and why do they want to do this today?"

"Harrison, remember we talked about this. I'm not disturbed that they want to come, but I am disturbed that they want to come today after calling you last night. Costello is getting a phone call from me as soon as we hang up, but I think I know what is going on."

"What?" Harrison asked.

"Remember, your father has Andrew Spawn so irate that he can't see straight. At the same time, Spawn wants you and Claire to panic. He needs you to live in fear."

"Why is that?" Harrison questioned further.

"Think about it, Harrison. He wants to isolate your father as much as possible. To make that happen, he must divide your family. In other words, he needs you to stop communicating with him. He does that by turning you against your father. The more scared and angrier you become, the more he suspects you will blame your father for everything that has transpired."

"Understood," Harrison said.

"This is a tactic the government uses all the time. If they can isolate your father and take away his family – the people he loves most – then the expectation is that he will cooperate with them throughout this process."

"They don't know my father very well. He's not into his family," Harrison responded half-joking.

"They don't know the depth of your relationship but don't underestimate the tactic. If they can turn you, and possibly Victoria against him, they will have a considerable advantage over a man that is uncooperative up to this point."

"What do they get out of him other than fear?" he asked still probing for answers.

"Keep in mind that Spawn is convinced that your father still has millions of dollars hidden somewhere unrecovered. This may or may not be true, but they know if it does exist, this is the only way to get it. The government uses time and pressure to get the answers they need."

The method was working. Harrison was becoming extremely upset with his father. He was still dazed and confused, but now as his head began to clear, anger and resentment started to take their place.

Harrison had never stood up to his father. It wasn't so much that he allowed his dad to control him. Instead, Harrison tried to shake off his dad's controlling nature and not let it affect him. Truth be known, it wasn't working. In the past, Harrison tried to let things go, but he always harbored resentment. He said very little to Claire. Harrison mostly internalized his father's behavior. Now his emotions started to shift.

"So now what?" Harrison asked.

"Let Spawn come today and take the video. I'll be there to make sure he doesn't use more intimidating tactics to get his way."

"Fine. I need to rearrange my schedule." Harrison agreed.

"Get used to it. We have a long road ahead, and Costello and Spawn won't let up anytime soon." Eckles added, "I'm calling Costello and chewing him out for his client's antics. That was bullshit, and it can't happen again."

Eckles and Harrison agreed to schedule the house visit for late afternoon so Harrison's entire day wouldn't be interrupted. That meant he would be thinking about a home visit from the IRS all day as opposed to focusing on his customers.

It also frustrated him that Spawn would only get a slap on the wrist for calling him. He was sure that Costello would reinforce the message to his IRS client.

Realistically, Costello would probably give Spawn a wink, and they would both have a good laugh. They had the high ground, and there was nothing the Marks could do except cooperate, as much as it hurt.

The day went surprisingly fast. Eckles arrived at the house ahead of the IRS agents, which was strategic to show Spawn they were prepared. He wouldn't catch them off guard again.

It was also to make sure Harrison was in the right frame of mind. His attitude and cooperation along with his father's cooperation were needed to get out from under the government's thumb. Whether Harrison wanted to hear it or not, it was a collaborative effort.

Spawn would arrive 35 minutes late. Eckles anticipated he would do this to show who was in control.

"Let him have his power trip, Harrison," she said. "This gives us time to talk. Believe it or not, you and Claire will get through this and be ok."

Greetings were exchanged awkwardly at the door. Eckles spoke on behalf of Harrison while pointing Spawn to the end of the hall.

The little pug bounced around the house with the special agent, not understanding that her master would like her to bite him on the leg. Spawn bent over to pet the animal hoping it would go away but that only encouraged her. As a result, Zoe ended up in the entire video that showcased every room in the single-level home, including the basement.

The entire experience was frustrating to Harrison. He felt violated. Eckles picked up on her client's disdain.

"Remember why they are here. Don't let them get to you," she whispered.

She was right. As they captured the video, they flexed their muscle to put stress on the young couple.

It was working. Harrison was just thankful that Claire was at work. This would have upset his wife for days. Even further, he should be the punching bag. For this reason, he felt more animosity toward Andrew Spawn.

After recording the inside of the house, it was time to go outside. In typical fashion, Zoe was the first one out the door.

With the iPad in his hand and the record button on, Spawn walked around the side of the house.

"Damn it," he shouted angrily. "I just stepped in dog shit."

Harrison did his best to keep a straight face. It was difficult, but he managed.

Spawn did his best to wipe the bottom of his shoe on cleaner grass, but it was still caked to the sides of the shoe.

"Can you get me a paper towel or something?" he yelled at Harrison.

Without saying a word, Harrison walked back into the house as if he was going to retrieve something to help the arrogant Spawn.

Harrison did not return. He stayed in the house laughing and knowing the agent was walking around the remainder of the house smelling like crap. He remained out of Spawn's view, but Harrison watched as they circled the house. Eckles stayed with the agents but lagged behind – likely due to the smell.

Ten minutes later, they were ready to leave. Harrison stayed inside out of view, but he could still see the conversation in the driveway. It appeared Spawn was holding out hope that Harrison would return with something to wipe his shoe before he left. It wasn't going to happen.

Finally, Spawn and his guys got in the car and backed out of the driveway with dog poop still stuck to his shoe.

TWENTY

"Gray hair is a crown of splendor;
it is attained by a righteous life."

A FEW WEEKS LATER, THE MARKS PUT THE BOAT AWAY FOR THE winter and disassembled the 75-foot awning from the patio. The sunshine was replaced with gray skies and windy days.

Now into the third trimester, Harrison and Claire continued as best they could. Molly Eckles shared with them that Costello was looking at a few dates for the deposition. The stress mounted for Claire and Harrison.

Harrison spent more time in his office reading online news articles related to his father. Each day he found new articles providing an update, but even those were beginning to slow down.

Attorneys from opposing sides negotiated behind the scenes to determine if Harlan Marks would take a deal or insist on having his day in court.

Claire continued to stay with her routine. Once she came home from work and changed clothes, she ate dinner and retreated to the bedroom.

She was past cooking meals. After standing on her feet all day, she looked forward to sprawling on the mattress. She was so uncomfortable at work and now sat on a donut cushion to relieve pressure on her tailbone. Lying in bed was a luxury.

The dog jumped up to join her. Zoe was always looking for a warm body.

Claire focused on the growing child inside and often wondered who the baby would resemble. She said a quick prayer asking only for a healthy baby and resumed rubbing her stomach, hoping for a foot or a hand to push back.

The child didn't disappoint. Claire gave a hearty laugh causing the baby to kick and push from the inside.

"Harrison, come here," she yelled happily at the top of her voice.

Harrison, uncertain of the situation, made the walk to the other end of the house.

"Feel my stomach," she exclaimed. "The baby is doing crazy things!"

Harrison crawled next to his wife and placed his hand on her stomach. Sure enough, the baby continued to tumble and kick. It was one of the few lighthearted moments the couple experienced in a long time.

They smiled at one another while Zoe jumped in the middle for attention.

At that moment, Claire's phone rang. She looked at the incoming number and recognized the name.

"Hi, Mom," Claire answered.

She was happy to speak to a friendly voice and welcomed the distraction to talk about something other than legal issues.

Harrison stood up to head back to his office and made it to the doorway before Claire screamed, "Oh my God."

He turned around to see the shock on her face. Harrison drew closer to understand what was wrong.

Claire began to cry and dropped the phone. Harrison picked it up and placed it to his ear.

"Lorraine, what's going on?"

"Harrison, I'm so sorry to tell you both, but Grandpa Ron has died."

Two weeks earlier, Claire's 79-year-old grandpa climbed a ladder to remove leaves from the spouting. Unfortunately, he fell from a 10-foot ladder and broke his collarbone.

The family was relieved to hear that he was going to be ok. However, the injury triggered a more serious medical issue that led to heart failure.

"Oh, no," Harrison said. "What happened?"

Lorraine explained the best she could while trying to hold her emotions together.

He was experiencing pain in his arm, shoulder and chest. Claire's father received the call and drove him to the emergency room. Grandpa Ron collapsed in the hallway. Harrison heard the part about congestive heart failure but nothing more. His mind turned to ask what else could go wrong.

Claire looked to her husband for answers. Harrison was overwhelmed by one more thing that he couldn't fix. His life and Claire's were falling apart.

At some point during the conversation, Harrison hung up when he heard the funeral was next week. Claire's mom would contact them with details later.

After much crying, Claire was finally able to fall asleep.

Problems began to mount. The upcoming birth of a child faded as they faced more devastating news.

Harrison lay in bed with his emotions building.

God, what are you doing to me? he questioned silently.

As a teenager, Harrison felt a connection with God and remembered that moment in college. He believed in the Gospel that Jesus was the true Savior.

But now he found himself questioning if God *was* good. *Didn't God know Harrison could use some intervention?*

Harrison recalled attending Sunday School as a child, *God was good all the time, and all the time God was good.*

Was this true? This period in his life certainly didn't feel good. *What was God's purpose to let him and Claire suffer?*

The questions mounted as he stared quietly at the dark ceiling. He believed he deserved better than what God was offering. God was taking away the joy of an expectant child. He questioned, *Why me?*, because other couples didn't have to put up with this crap.

Harrison thought back to his mom and dad's divorce. His mother found every reason to be gone during the evening hours. It was enough to destroy a man like his father. Still, the pain inflicted upon Harrison felt worse. His mom was absent as a teenager. His dad was absent as an adult.

Now, God felt absent.

Claire's alarm sounded at 6 a.m., and she rolled over to find her husband staring at the ceiling. She knew it was a difficult night.

"How was your night?" Claire asked.

"Not great. I'm sorry about your grandpa."

Claire appreciated the sentiment but sensed Harrison's mind was elsewhere.

"Did you sleep?" she asked.

"No," was his only response.

He got out of bed and got ready for work.

TWENTY-ONE

"The path of life leads upward for the wise,
to keep him from going down to the grave."

THE DAY OF THE FUNERAL WAS MIXED WITH SADNESS AND JOY. IT was the first time the family had been together in years.

How strange. The saddest part of the funeral wasn't the death of a family member, but that it took the death of a family member to get family together, Harrison thought.

Before the funeral, the family gathered at her grandfather's house. It was unusual to see family members posing for pictures and primping, but then again, Harrison's family was nothing like Claire's family. He would have enjoyed having a larger family.

In the kitchen, family members downed an alcoholic drink to calm the nerves. A distant cousin even reached into her purse and washed down a Xanax with cheap whiskey.

Harrison walked to the back yard to be alone. He could only think about himself and the Assistant United States Attorney David Costello and his IRS sidekick Andrew Spawn.

He looked at his watch and knew it was about time to leave for the service. Harrison walked to the patio door, and it was locked. He didn't see anyone inside. Harrison quickly walked around to the front of the house to see all the cars were gone.

They left him at the house. Unfortunately, he and Claire rode with her parents, so his car wasn't accessible. Even so, why didn't Claire notice that her husband wasn't in the car sitting next to her?

Really God? he mocked while looking up to the sky.

He had two choices. Walk a half-mile to Claire's parents to pick up his car or walk a half-mile to the funeral home. He chose the latter.

Dressed in his best blue suit, he began the journey. On an overcast day, it began to rain.

Isn't this just perfect? he thought.

Harrison began to laugh but wanted to cry. He was between two emotions. He knew this would be funny if it happened to someone other than him.

He cut through yards trying to stay under trees as much as possible. Soggy, embarrassed, and angry, he arrived at the funeral home 15 minutes later.

He caught the stares of every family member as he walked through the door and straight to his wife. She looked at him for a moment and then burst out laughing.

It was the first time he saw her laugh in months. Although he was happy to see it, it also upset him that she was laughing at him for an incident that she caused in the first place.

"Why did you leave me?"

"I thought you were in another car," she said as she smirked and tried not to laugh.

The ceremony was about to begin. Harrison took his seat in the second row with his wife.

"Do you want to go to the restroom and dry off?"

A defiant Harrison glared at his wife and looked back to Pastor Doug.

Claire's parents glanced back at him a few times and managed to crack a smile at their drenched son-in-law.

Pastor Bob began. Harrison drifted in and out of the sermon. Messages about God and His promise fell on deaf ears.

Harrison wasn't denying God's existence, but he was denying that God is good all the time.

Pastor Bob continued, "And we know that for those who love God all things work together for good, for those who are called according to his purpose," citing Romans 8:28.

Harrison quietly doubted and thought *it sounds like total bullshit.*

He remained silent as he scanned the room.

Pastor Bob reinforced, "Sometimes life doesn't turn out the way we think it should. At times, circumstances beyond our control enter our life and put us in a difficult situation. We don't always see a way out. These moments cause struggle and pain. Yes, bad things happen to the people of God, but Paul shares that all things work together for the good of God."

The pastor brought it back to the death of a loved one.

He shared that Ronald Rice was a Godly man. And while he was elderly and nearing the end of his time on earth, the death was unexpected and sudden. Pastor Bob assured his listeners that not only did God have a purpose for everyone, but he promised life eternal for those who declared Jesus as their Savior. As humans relegated to this earth, we don't have the big picture.

"But until the end, you have to endure all the crap here on earth," Harrison leaned over and said to Claire.

For Harrison, it was easy to be angry with God. A life of doing good and occasional prayer seemed adequate. He believed all the stories of the Bible. He certainly believed in the Gospel and thought it was *The Greatest Story Ever Told.*

Could all this be a lie? Could the Bible be nothing more than stories collected in a book? Was it fictional? He pondered this as the pastor continued with the service.

He questioned why he believed in a god that allowed such cruel things to happen to good people. Harrison wondered if he believed in God because others told him he should believe. Was it simply a popular way to think because it aligned with others around him? Or did he have an authentic connection with God regardless of their belief?

If he didn't go to church as a young boy, would he have been a believer? Then again, should he care if he was a believer or not? He didn't focus on God as much as he should, but his life turned out pretty good until now. Still, he had a career that paid well, a house on a lake, a wife that loved him, and a baby on the way.

He knew others who never spoke about God and would never consider going to church. These people seemed to have as much, or more than him. *Did God matter?*

It certainly didn't appear to be true. So far, Christianity appeared to offer no advantages over those that weren't nearly as faithful.

Harrison did his best to put those thoughts aside. Ronald Rice was now laid to rest, and he had bigger worries knocking on his door. He turned his thoughts again to his situation.

On the ride home Claire remained silent while hoping that her husband would speak to her. She felt alone. Week after week, Harrison was distracted by his own thoughts. She started to feel as if she was being robbed of the joy of pregnancy…and marriage.

She forced smiles and offered a polite answer when others asked about the due date. She missed the connection with her husband who seemed to forget they were about to become a family.

Small arguments turned into big arguments. Big arguments resulted in hours of silence and resentment, mostly from Claire. Harrison was neglecting her as a wife and a mother-to-be. She needed him to be her rock as he had always been.

Things were different now. She became too tired to fight. Getting him to come out of his isolation required something more than she could provide. If only the issue with his dad would go away, then things could return to normal. However, Harrison wasn't going to return to her without first solving the problem – that's how he functioned.

She missed the joy of a new day and how she used to look forward to another day with her husband, colleagues, and friends. Now, waking up in the morning meant another day of dreaded challenges.

Claire was not one to place blame, but this was certainly not her fault. Harlan wasn't her family even though her mother always said, "Remember, when you marry someone, you not only marry that person, you also marry the family."

She didn't mean it to this extent, Claire now thought to herself.

Harlan was a problem. Hell, Harlan was always a problem. He was a distraction even in his absence. She was scared he would also become a distraction to her as a mother and that was crossing the line. She wouldn't allow it.

For Claire Marks, she was ready to break the chains.

TWENTY-TWO

"He who finds a wife finds what is good and receives favor."

IT WAS NOW NOVEMBER, AND CLAIRE WAS IN HER EIGHTH MONTH OF pregnancy. For her, every day went by slowly, and every day felt like a week. Adding to this, her husband was preparing for a full basketball officiating schedule.

The Lamaze classes scheduled twice a week helped the couple connect on an emotional level. Harrison didn't take it too seriously, but he and Claire always stopped for dinner after the classes making it worth the effort. He understood his role wasn't as demanding as it was for Claire.

At the same time, Harrison never lacked confidence in his ability, even when it came to tasks where he had no experience.

This will be easy, he thought.

He often joked aloud, "I could land a jumbo jet in a crisis if needed."

Although his confidence was never in doubt, it was a double-edged sword. It was a characteristic that attracted Claire, but it led to Harrison believing he could do everything alone.

He didn't like to ask for help. Handling matters on his own proved to be more efficient and less complicated. Also, Harrison enjoyed the independence even if the outcome ended up poorly.

But as time progressed, he struggled. He began to question himself daily. If he couldn't help himself, how could he help Claire?

There were no clear answers, and uncertainty felt like a rain cloud hovering overhead. No one could relate to what he was experiencing – not even

Claire. The fact that he had no brothers or sisters to share the burden didn't help.

"You need to talk to someone," Claire suggested out of the blue one evening during dinner.

"What do you mean?"

"You are internalizing everything. I know you're worried, and you're not ok."

"I have you."

"Yes, but you don't talk to me."

"I'm just trying to figure it out and wondering what the future holds."

Harrison paused, then realized his mistake. "Please know it has nothing to do with you or the baby."

Claire smiled another perfect smile. "I know. That's why you need to talk to someone."

"Who?"

"Schedule some time with Pastor Bob."

"In Madison? How am I going to do that? He's two hours away?"

"You could find a way. He's somebody you know and trust, and I'm sure he knows our story."

Claire was right. Harrison was certain Pastor Bob knew the story of his father. He also knew Harrison since Claire's parents lived across the street from the parsonage.

Claire noticed Harrison contemplating the idea, but this would be a process to convince her husband. She planted the seed. She knew it would take time.

Now into December, Harrison was in full swing with his officiating season. It was typical for him to have two or three games a week, but this season was different. He had two games during the week and then a Friday and Saturday night game. Another game was often wedged in on Saturday afternoon to accommodate the girls' schedule.

This schedule was not by mistake. Harrison told Claire they needed the money to support attorney bills. However, he also kept busy since being home meant he would think about his dad, his grandmother and now the future of their home.

The young couple knew they could stay at the house, but knew they were going to owe money to the government. There was a chance they could win their case, but even so, attorney bills were mounting. Putting money into a retirement account was out of the question since their money had to be used elsewhere.

Harrison and Claire worked hard to build their retirement savings since the start of their marriage. But now, they put that on hold while they paid an attorney and the IRS for a criminal matter beyond their control. Harrison was infuriated.

He could only picture the $50,000 dining room table and other valuable items still sitting inside his father's house that would easily cover his expenses.

For Claire, money was a factor. However, she saw everything occurring on a deeper level. From the very beginning, she had a front-row seat to the "Harlan and Victoria Show".

The houses, the vacations, the clothes, and most importantly, the lack of family priorities left her husband to internalize his emotions. Now Harlan pulled her into the spotlight with his criminal activity, while she and Harrison missed out on the celebration of her pregnancy.

Now, she felt the eyes of Indianapolis on her. She wasn't entirely wrong as all the people in Claire's life knew her story. The neighbors in the subdivision, co-workers, and her family all knew her story. Only a few friends took pity upon her, and she hated it.

Claire would often take weekend trips back to Madison. Spending time with her parents offered her an escape from reality.

Harrison became an easy target for Claire. Her frustration was placed with Harlan and Victoria, but it was directed at Harrison.

Her resentment mounted watching her husband continue to be the obedient son and grandson, and not the supportive husband. Claire believed it was best to be out of the house.

She found peace attending church with her family. On many occasions, she heard something she wished her husband could hear.

Now, nearly two weeks before Christmas and a baby due on December 27th, the Marks knew they had little time remaining as a couple.

Harrison was excited to become a father, but having a baby didn't seem real. The child needed to be present and he needed to hold it to make it real.

For Claire, she became a mother the day she found out she was pregnant. The sentiment grew deeper every time she felt the baby kick.

Harrison's focus on his father diminished when he thought about being a dad. His wife was excited to see the change, even though his evening conversations with his grandmother were still a struggle.

Mimi called each night, and she was often in tears. She had no one else to talk to during the day and looked forward to her calls with Harrison. By the time they were able to talk, she had worked herself into a meltdown.

She blamed herself for not being a good mother. She blamed Elaine Hansen for letting the business get so out of hand. She also blamed Harrison for not being a supportive son to Harlan.

She blamed everyone except Harlan. According to her, he was innocent. She wanted the attention focused on him and didn't understand why his attorney wasn't doing more to help.

"He's guilty," Harrison finally interrupted.

"Oh, damn you," she stated emphatically. "This has been a witch hunt from the beginning, and they are only looking to make an example of him and make a name for themselves."

Harrison expected a rebuttal but didn't think the old lady had it in her to respond with such force. He should have known better. Mimi would gladly sacrifice Harrison and anyone else to make it easier for her son, regardless of his wrongdoing. Anyway, she was simply parroting what her son was telling her.

She continued to tell Harrison each night about the battles within the apartment complex. Residents knew she was Harlan's mother. They often asked how he was doing, and if the accusations were true.

"You just mind your own business", she would snap.

Harrison wasn't so concerned about upsetting her anymore. The challenge of dealing with other people mounted while he also held down a career. He had to prioritize his life. He knew that pulling his grandmother out of the ashes every night could no longer be a priority.

He was about to become a father.

TWENTY-THREE

"A cheerful look brings joy to the heart,
and good news gives health to the bones."

WITH ONLY TWO WEEKS AWAY FROM CHRISTMAS, CLAIRE'S ALARM sounded declaring another workday.

She pulled herself out of bed as she struggled with exhaustion. Although Claire didn't experience typical morning sickness like other pregnant women, she was exhausted.

Extreme exhaustion in the morning often lasted until lunch. It proved to be a nice distraction from the ongoing pain in her tailbone while trying to sit at her desk.

An hour later, Claire emerged from the bathroom and walked to the bed to kiss her husband goodbye. Harrison remained asleep.

She whispered his name, and he rolled over. As he did, she managed to poke him directly in the right eye while reaching for his face.

Harrison felt a pain that he had never felt before. He placed his hand over his eye, but there was nothing he could do to relieve the pain. Although Claire pulled back quickly, Harrison still felt like a needle sat square in the center of his eye.

It was so bad he canceled his morning appointment to find an eye doctor who could take an emergency appointment.

The doctor determined that his wife severely scratched his cornea, and it would take days, if not weeks, to heal.

He now functioned with an eye patch throughout the remaining days to block out the light. The pain was most extreme when opening his eye for the first time each morning. The cornea would tear after Harrison's eye was closed for a long period. Early morning visits to the eye doctor became a new daily schedule to receive drops that allowed him to function throughout the day.

After a few days, Harrison got used to the eye patch. He only removed it in the evening when he and Claire turned off the bedroom lights.

The little pug snored loudly and Claire had to nudge her to quiet her down. This, too, became routine.

As 11 p.m. came and went, they found themselves awake. Harrison was in pain because of his eye, and Claire was in pain because of another human being growing inside. Harrison was convinced that he had it worse than his wife.

"What does your day look like tomorrow?" Claire asked quietly.

Harrison never had time to answer when he heard Claire exclaim, "Oh my God, my water broke."

He sat up and turned on the light. He could do nothing more than stare at his wife in disbelief.

"What did you do?" he demanded to know.

Claire kept still on the bed evaluating her situation. She didn't bother to answer such a stupid question.

Harrison recalled all he learned from Lamaze.

"I remember them saying we have plenty of time. You're supposed to get in the shower to try to relax."

He flipped on the bathroom light and turned on the shower.

"Get in here," Harrison called to Claire. "You have to relax," he shouted in a voice opposite of remaining calm.

In a fog, Claire prepared for a shower. Harrison was right. They should have plenty of time to get to the hospital.

"Jesus, we don't have a hospital bag packed," he cried out.

"Well, no," Claire exclaimed. "I'm not due to have this kid for another two weeks."

Harrison grabbed a duffle bag and gathered every bottle of makeup he could find in Claire's ensemble. Eyeliner, concealer, and lipstick were all included, but he unknowingly failed to provide a toothbrush, toothpaste, dental floss, or contact solution.

"It's happening!" Claire yelled from inside the shower. "We don't have time."

She turned off the shower and felt the baby dropping. After attempting to dry off, she tried to get dressed while still wet.

Harrison went to the closet to get coats. He could only see out of one eye. Although the adrenalin kicked in, Harrison was feeling the sharp pain. He tried to focus.

Claire managed to put on clothes even though her hair and body were wet. It didn't matter. They had to go.

Harrison pulled out of the driveway and knew that the hospital was 10 minutes away. It was nearly midnight, and thankfully, traffic wasn't an issue.

"I think I'm ok," Claire whispered while trying to breathe through the pain.

Harrison wasn't buying it. He sped through town and blew through stoplights. He jumped the railroad tracks, and the company car went airborne.

Claire groaned in pain. "Slow down. You're going to kill all three of us," she shouted.

She felt another contraction and quickly changed her mind. "Ok, maybe you do need to hurry."

Harrison squealed the tires pulling into the hospital. He hit the brakes in front of the emergency room entrance while honking the horn several times to get someone's attention.

He got out of the car and ran around to get Claire.

An orderly came outside with a wheelchair.

"We're having a baby," Harrison yelled.

A nurse heard the response and came to help. They ushered Claire into the chair, and they wheeled her up the elevator into a delivery room. Harrison followed with the duffle bag in hand.

Claire told the nurse to contact Dr. Shale. She soon found out that, unfortunately, Dr. Shale was delivering another baby at a hospital across town. Claire would have to deliver to an intern who was hoping to get some sleep.

After a thorough evaluation, the nurse and intern determined it was too late for an epidural. Claire had to go through this birth without a pain killer.

Contractions stayed consistent for the next few hours. After several hours, another nurse walked into the delivery room and asked Harrison if his car was parked in the emergency drop-off area.

"Oh, damn. Are you kidding me?" he asked in disbelief.

"It's still running," mentioned the nurse.

Harrison looked at Claire, and she managed a giggle. He raced downstairs and moved the car after the doctor confirmed he should have time.

When he returned, the delivery room was in full swing, and Dr. Shale was in attendance. She assumed the catcher's position in front of Claire.

"What's going on?" he asked as if he didn't know.

"You're about to become parents," the doctor reminded him.

Twenty minutes later, Claire gave birth to a 6 lb. 9 oz healthy baby girl at 4:32 a.m. on December 16th.

Harrison beamed with delight as the nurses cleaned and wrapped her.

Claire came through the delivery without complications. Soon they were in the room alone with their daughter.

The couple had a name picked out for a boy and a girl. They now welcomed Rebecca Rose Marks. They would call her Becca.

After they both had a chance to hold her, they knew they had to call their parents.

Claire went first. Her parents made a point to come up as soon as possible that morning.

Harrison picked up the phone to call his mother. She answered and said, "That's great, honey," and promptly hung up the phone.

6 a.m. was too early for his mother. He would have to call her back later to remind her she was a grandmother.

After a few hours, Harrison kissed his wife and his daughter. He went home to shower. He also printed pink fliers to place in mailboxes. Everyone in the Hidden Shores community needed to know.

He returned later that morning with Mimi, who was thrilled to be a great-grandmother. It was a nice distraction for her to focus on something that brought joy.

She reminded her grandson on the ride to the hospital, "Today's the day that your grandfather died. Now December 16th can be a good day again. It seems ironic, doesn't it?"

Harrison was stunned to hear that news. He wasn't sure if it was irony or something more spiritual. A day that brought heartache for many years was redeemed by the birth of a great-granddaughter. He considered the possibility of God making it happen. It didn't seem like a coincidence.

Then, Mimi spoke again, disrupting his thoughts, "I called Victoria to let her know we have a new member of the family."

"Ok."

Harrison knew he needed to call Victoria at some point. He was thankful Mimi saved him the hassle. Harrison was hopeful Victoria wouldn't show.

Another call to Harrison's mother verified that she didn't remember the earlier phone call. JoAnn and Fred arrived at the hospital shortly after hearing the news and stayed all afternoon. She and Harrison's step-father were kind enough to take Mimi home so Harrison could be with his family.

Much to his surprise, Victoria arrived at the hospital shortly after dinner. Her visit was unexpected.

Harrison stared at Victoria, trying to let her know that he wasn't fooled by her presence. Claire carried most of the conversation.

Victoria held Becca awkwardly, showing how little experience she had with babies. Claire watched her closely.

They hadn't talked in a long time. The visit to the hospital had nothing to do with the love Victoria had for her family.

She left after a brief stay, and it was a deep sigh of relief for the Marks.

"Is it weird that she came to visit?" Claire asked.

Harrison was prepared for this exact question.

"She's still on the hook as an unindicted co-conspirator, and she knows Mimi and I are still in contact with my dad."

"So."

"So, she's hoping when we see my dad again, we'll tell him she visited. That will make him happy, and Victoria will stay in his good graces."

"I guess so."

"Remember, my dad is in the middle of a plea bargain with the IRS, and Victoria is positioning herself to be the beneficiary of that plea bargain."

"She's playing the game," Claire concluded.

"Of course. She doesn't want my dad to think she's not 100% invested in our family. It will cost her if Dad thinks she's not going to be around once this ends. This visit solidifies her standing with my father. She's just buying time," Harrison stated.

"He could have included us in that plea bargain, don't you think?" Claire inquired, although she knew the answer to that question.

"Sure."

Harlan played his cards, anticipating Harrison would always remain loyal. Even with the younger Marks' mounting attorney bills, an upcoming deposition, and potentially a stiff payment to the IRS, Harlan took a gamble on his son.

Victoria was the wild card. Therefore, the strategy centered on easing her burden. She pulled all the right strings with her husband when he was most vulnerable.

She didn't visit him in jail because she claimed it was too much of a hardship. She fed him a sob story each time he called collect to tell him how she couldn't sleep at night because she was having terrible nightmares. She claimed Marks Medical Supply employees were calling her with threats, although she couldn't provide Harlan names or phone numbers. Overall, she did a great job playing the victim, and it was about to pay off.

"I can't stand her," Claire said. "I don't want her around Becca ever again."

Harrison agreed.

It was time to re-focus on Becca, who was starting to fuss.

After one more night in the hospital, Claire and Becca were released.

Harrison arrived early that morning with clothes for his wife since he also forgot to include those in the duffle bag.

Claire was anxious to get home and settle into a routine. She was scheduled to take the next six weeks off from work and would cherish every second.

Becca fell asleep in the baby carrier on the ride home. They carried their daughter into the house and placed her on the couch.

Zoe bounced with excitement. The little dog jumped on and off the couch, attempting to lick the new arrival. She tried every which way to get to Becca. Zoe was more excited about the baby than the adults.

Harrison and Claire stood and stared at Becca from a distance while the dog continued her antics. It was safe to say reality set in, and they were a little overwhelmed.

"Now what?" Harrison asked.

TWENTY-FOUR

"There is a way that seems right to a man,
but in the end it leads to death."

HARRISON WAS A PROUD FATHER. HE LEARNED QUICKLY THAT ALL people love babies, and he wanted to show his daughter to everyone.

It also meant taking her to meet her grandfather in the downtown jail a few weeks later.

Claire wasn't thrilled about the idea of her daughter entering the facility, but she knew it would be a lost cause trying to talk her husband out of it.

Mimi went along.

They arrived earlier than usual, knowing Becca needed to be patted down since it wasn't unusual to see drugs go unnoticed through the security checkpoint. Harrison recalled one visitor swallowing a small packet of cocaine on the sidewalk only to regurgitate and hand it to an inmate when the guards weren't looking. Cameras were situated around the room, but that didn't stop drug trafficking and other contraband.

As expected, Becca received a search. Harrison handed his daughter over to the female guard, who allowed him to follow her to a back room where she undressed the infant and checked inside her diaper.

It disturbed Harrison even though the guard continued to assure him it was standard policy.

The elevator arrived on the 4th floor, and each visitor took their seat. Harrison was amused that Mimi finally caught on to the protocol after a couple of months.

Harlan and the other inmates waited patiently behind a set of bars that eventually opened once the visitors settled at their respective tables.

Harrison handed Becca over to his father. Harlan smiled as he stared at Becca, who had finally fallen asleep.

Mimi, once again, sat silently and enjoyed being in the presence of her son.

Harrison felt a heavy-hearted emotion come over him. A grandfather should not meet his grandchild this way. He was sad for himself and his father.

His father suffered greater consequences, but Harrison realized his dad wouldn't get to experience the joy of being a grandfather to his daughter.

It was one more thing his father had taken from him – one more thing contributing to an overall bitterness that brewed for a long time – even before his father had been arrested.

"What has Hausmann shared lately?" Harrison asked, hoping for good news.

"Haven't heard from him, which tells me things are moving slow. I've been awaiting a visit from him because I want an update on Victoria. She has a different attorney, so maybe he doesn't know either."

Harrison was disturbed by that comment, and it needed to be unpacked.

"What do you mean?" Harrison responded. "Don't you know how she's doing?"

"Well, no. She takes my calls each week, but doesn't like to talk. She's scared, Harrison. She's feeling alone and doesn't know what to do next. I've tried to offer her hope, but it's hard to do when I'm behind bars."

"Doesn't she come to see you?"

"No. You should know. Sunday is the only day for visitation, and you two are the only people that come. She says it makes her uncomfortable and causes too much anxiety. I can understand."

"I can't," Harrison snapped. "This is uncomfortable for all of us."

Harlan didn't respond, and Harrison took the opportunity to continue.

"So, what's going on with Victoria's case?" Harrison knew she had a different attorney and understood since she was named as an unindicted co-conspirator. He wanted to know if the attorneys were working together or if each had their specific client's interest in mind.

"Well, we're both fighting for the same goal, but the attorneys seem to be working independently. I've asked her how her case is progressing, but she doesn't seem to know much."

"So, is your attorney and her attorney working for the best individual outcomes rather than the best outcome for you as a couple?"

"Well, yes, I guess. Ultimately, Victoria and I want the same thing. We're mostly in this together."

Harrison laughed. "Are you kidding me? She hasn't come to visit you. She doesn't like to talk to you on the phone. We don't hear from her," he said pointing, back and forth between himself and Mimi, "and you think she has your best interest in mind?"

"Sure," Harlan said with substantial doubt.

Harrison sat back and glared at his father. The man that was so good at controlling people thought he could still do it from inside a jail cell.

Did he think Victoria was doing anything other than trying to save her ass?, Harrison wondered.

His father was out of touch with reality. His hope had transitioned to desperation.

The younger Marks decided to let it go. He would have to weigh the consequences of resuming the conversation. Harrison knew that Harlan could panic and share his son's concerns with Victoria during one of his weekly five-minute phone calls.

For now, Harrison needed Victoria to play nice to ensure she didn't complicate matters. There was no telling what she might share with her attorney regarding Harrison's involvement. She might spin his summer employment to be more than packaging products for shipment. For now, he needed harmony.

Harlan saw his son piecing together a story he didn't want to be true. The last thing the old man needed was another reason to stay awake at night.

"I know she's just stressed," he said, trying to convince Harrison as much as himself.

"She went to Chicago with Joni for a few days to get away. By the way, I need you to do something for me."

"Ok," said Harrison.

"I want you to get my dad's diamond ring. I mentioned it to Victoria, but I think she's too preoccupied with everything. I'm afraid it's going to be one more thing the government will try to take. They are preparing to auction some expensive items in the house, and I know they are doing a walk-through next week. I'm afraid they will seize the ring if they find it. I want you to have it, I want it to be safe."

Mimi gave the diamond ring to her son when he was 18 years old. She kept it in a safe until he was old enough to take the responsibility. It was the only heirloom Harlan had to remind him of his father. Keeping the ring safe meant keeping the memory of his father safe.

Harrison understood its importance and value. "Ok, where is it?"

"It's in a small fireproof box that I keep in my closet. I don't think Victoria knows where to find it. If you could, go get it this week. I know Victoria is gone, but she won't mind. I'll tell her the next time I talk to her," his father added.

Harrison listened. His dad thought the authorities were the most dangerous to the ring, last valued at $8,000. Harrison was more concerned about Victoria getting her hands on it. He also knew he needed to get in the house before his father advised Victoria. Harrison didn't think she would agree to the plan at all. If she found out before he got the ring, nobody would see it again.

For very different reasons, they both agreed the ring needed to be with Harrison.

Harlan gave Harrison the security code to the house. Without his cell phone, or pen and paper, he put it to memory.

Harlan handed Becca to Harrison when it was time to leave. Harrison was convinced his father was still living in a fantasy world, but that had to wait for another day.

He took his grandmother home. Harrison and Mimi only exchanged a few words until they arrived at her apartment complex.

"Are you going to go to your father's house to get the ring?" she asked.

He was frustrated that she didn't say, "Thank you for taking me today."

Harrison showed his disapproval giving her an abrupt, "Probably."

"When? You know Harrison, your father is counting on you."

"Well, I've been counting on him for a long time, but look where that got me."

Mimi exited the car but not without scolding her grandson.

"He needs us right now, and you could show appreciation for the things that he has done for you. He didn't raise you to act selfishly."

His grandmother had no idea what she was saying. His father was the most selfish person in the world, and that's what caused this mess. Besides, she didn't raise her son to act like a criminal, but that certainly didn't stop him. *What did she have to say about that?*

He took a deep breath and swallowed to avoid speaking. To say that out loud would devastate Mimi.

"I'll see you next week," she said as she closed the door forcefully.

Harrison wasn't so sure about that statement. The weekends were getting stressful, and she wasn't making it easy.

TWENTY-FIVE

"But whoever listens to me will live in safety and be at ease, without fear of harm."

HARRISON DECIDED TO GO TO HIS FATHER'S HOUSE. HE WOULD GO after officiating a girls' basketball game the next evening. Harrison knew he had to get possession of the ring before Victoria returned from Chicago.

He told Claire what he was going to do, and she reluctantly shrugged her shoulders. There wasn't much to say once her husband made his decision. To ask him not to go meant an unnecessary argument neither of them needed.

The game went well Monday evening. After showering in the locker room, he headed toward the Geist Reservoir home.

Harrison meandered through the subdivision to the Marks' estate.

He pulled into the U-shaped drive and entered through the garage door, which he knew was always unlocked. If an intruder knew where to enter, they could at least get away with a Jaguar – not a bad deal.

The Jag was missing, and Harrison recalled it was confiscated during the seizure. Victoria was relegated to driving the Jeep, and it made Harrison laugh out loud.

He punched in the set of numbers his father gave him to get in the house.

"What if that bitch changed the security code?"

He pressed *Enter* and the house alarm began to sound. The pitch was ear-piercing and Harrison knew it could be heard throughout the neighborhood.

He froze for an instant. His eyes widened, and his heart started to race. He wanted to sprint to his car and leave the neighborhood as soon as possible. It was the smart plan. In doing so, however, the diamond ring would likely never be recovered.

The house alarm continued to shriek. In his frenzy, the shrill appeared to get louder and louder.

Harrison grew disoriented from the deafening sound. Forcing himself to focus, he had a decision to make – leave immediately and never recover the diamond ring or take a chance.

Determined, he pushed the door open leading inside the house and darted for the master bedroom. He flipped the bedroom light switch to locate the two closets.

"Dammit. Which one is his?" Harrison shouted.

He was sure the police were en route. Harrison knew that he made a terrible mistake coming into the house. For a brief moment, he thought he should leave.

I'm committed now, Harrison thought. He told himself he needed to be in his car within the next 30 seconds.

He picked the closet on the right and turned on the light.

"Jesus Christ!" he exclaimed as he walked into Victoria's closet. He had a 50/50 shot at guessing the right closet, and he was dismayed that he chose wrong. He didn't have time for mistakes.

Harrison bolted to the next closet and went down on the floor to the back corner.

Buried under a pile of shoeboxes he found a small fireproof box.

Harrison wasted no time securing the box, scampering out of the house and back to his car.

More than one minute passed since the alarm initially sounded. Outside lights flipped on from other homes as neighbors checked the commotion.

Anybody looking from their house could see a black SUV leaving the subdivision.

Nothing suspicious here, Harrison mocked himself.

He drove out of the subdivision and scanned the main road for flashing lights barreling toward his direction. He needed to wait for cars to pass. He didn't see police cars, but he needed to wait for oncoming traffic to pass. He felt trapped by cars coming from both directions. An otherwise quiet road was now blocking his escape as he felt his anxiety soar.

The last car turned into the subdivision. Harrison watched his hands tremble on the steering wheel as he considered that the car could be an unmarked police car. He caught the eye of the other driver. The older lady glared at him realizing his impatience to pull onto the road. Harrison breathed in as he tried to get relief, then made a sharp left turn in the opposite direction of the police station.

With no other cars coming in his direction, he turned off his lights. Harrison never appreciated his rearview mirror more than now. Instantaneously, he noticed red flashing lights coming from behind. Harrison had no idea how much time passed since the alarm sounded.

"Please turn into the subdivision. Please turn," he said out loud.

The lights looked to be getting closer and closer as he continued driving in the dark. He now understood how his father might have felt when he outran the authorities only four months earlier.

As he anxiously continued to check the rearview mirror, headlights ahead caught his attention. The car coming toward him slammed on the brakes and laid on the horn as Harrison's SUV drifted into the opposite lane with no lights on.

Harrison pulled the steering wheel hard to the right and slammed on the brakes. Catching his breath and his bearings, he realized he had come upon an intersection.

After checking the mirror one more time, he couldn't see headlights approaching him.

Harrison turned his lights on and made a quick left as he scurried back to the main road to blend in with other travelers.

When he arrived home, Claire saw the look in her husband's eyes.

"What's wrong?" she asked.

After he shared the abbreviated version, she told him how she thought it was a bad idea.

"Thanks, Nostradamus," Harrison exclaimed sarcastically.

"What did you think would happen? You said yourself that Victoria is pretty sharp when it comes to looking out for herself."

Harrison said nothing. What could he say? Claire was right.

"You could have been arrested. Besides," she continued, "when are you going to start spending time at home instead of helping people who don't give a damn about us?"

Again, he knew it was true. Claire wasn't often abrupt, but when she spoke her mind, it was best to listen to her practical advice. It wouldn't be the last time he would hear from her.

Still, Harrison wanted no part of Claire's logic. He came to the same conclusion on the stressful ride home.

Another sleepless night meant another early morning. Harrison kissed and hugged his wife before leaving for work, then walked into the garage to open the overhead door. Before he got to his car, two police cars pulled in the driveway blocking his exit.

Claire saw the cars pull in and immediately came out of the house.

"Have they come to arrest you?" Claire asked in fear.

"No, just relax."

One of the officers asked Harrison if he was at the 10741 address on Sand Key Circle last night at precisely 9:42 p.m.?

Harrison seemed prepared.

"Yes, of course. But I left when the alarm sounded. Apparently, I entered the wrong code."

The officers seemed surprised Mr. Marks didn't flinch when they asked the question.

They continued, "Why were you there?"

Harrison launched into a story concerning the thermostat.

"When I visited my father yesterday at the jail, he told me his wife was in Chicago. He was concerned the thermostat was set too low since temperatures dropped below freezing this week. My father wanted me to check the thermostat setting so the pipes wouldn't freeze. He told me it had happened a couple of times. He was afraid this time they may burst, and no one would be around."

The officers didn't flinch either.

"We received a call from Victoria Marks. She was concerned you were attempting to break in during her absence. Is that accurate?

Harrison acted surprised. Claire was in shock.

"Of course not. As a matter of fact, I called Victoria to verify the code before I went to the house. She gave it to me, and we talked for about five minutes."

The officers were curious. "You spoke with her last night? What time?"

"Here's the stamp for the outgoing call," Harrison showed his phone to the men in blue.

"You said she gave you the code?"

After leaving the game, Harrison began to question his sanity for going to the house. During the drive to the Sand Key Circle address, he feared

Victoria might have changed the code after the house was raided sending her husband on the run.

He was also certain she would take the opportunity to cause trouble if she found out he tripped the alarm while attempting to get inside.

Harrison didn't trust Victoria with the ring. He didn't trust her with anything. She knew it was a family heirloom, and she knew how much it was worth. Harrison also knew she would take it to the pawnshop if she didn't already.

He needed to get the ring. If anybody was going to exchange it for cash, it was going to be him.

However, he also needed an alibi if the plan went wrong. Moments before entering the subdivision, Harrison called Victoria. Fortunately, she picked up on the third ring. Had she not, he would have aborted the plan.

"Hey, Victoria. How are you?" Harrison asked.

Victoria was surprised to receive a call from Harrison, but she picked up thinking it could be important.

He asked her about the trip to Chicago. He mentioned his dad shared some of the details the day before.

Once she found out Harrison was asking random questions, she waited for an opportunity to hang up. She didn't care for him and didn't want to spend any more time on the phone than necessary.

Harrison rambled on about Claire, Becca and the excitement of becoming a father.

"By the way, I never got the chance to thank you for stopping by the hospital last month. Claire and I appreciated your visit," he added.

He was ok with her short answers and unpleasantries. Harrison only wanted to keep her on the phone for a few minutes to make it look like they had a meaningful conversation.

Harrison kept Victoria on the line for five minutes. There was no mention of the security code and certainly no mention to get in her house to take his father's ring. It didn't matter. Harrison didn't need numbers, he only needed Victoria's time on the phone. Yes, Victoria provided the perfect alibi.

One officer looked at the time stamp and the length of the call on Harrison's phone. Harrison appeared to be telling the truth. Plus, the number the officer was given at the precinct matched Harrison's outgoing call to Victoria.

The second officer spoke, "The alarm sounded, and the security company called us immediately. We found out it was you when Victoria Marks identified you on the home security camera this morning."

"Well, that makes sense. Of course, it was me. Not only did I talk to her, but I was with my dad yesterday at the jail, which you already seem to know. I have nothing to hide."

Harrison knew the cameras in the jail were only visual and not wired for sound. He hoped the officers couldn't read lips.

"Why is Mrs. Marks concerned you were breaking in?"

Harrison chuckled as if he was expecting this question.

"Look, that woman is my step-mom who apparently hates me more than anyone. She's a co-conspirator in a multi-million-dollar crime, and she would push her mother down the stairs if it helped her situation."

Harrison knew Victoria was an unindicted co-conspirator, but co-conspirator sounded better.

"Why did you leave the scene?"

"First of all, boys, it wasn't a *scene*. It's still my father's house. Secondly, Victoria told me if I enter the number wrong to go ahead and leave. She told me the alarm would reset in five minutes. She made it seem like it wasn't a big deal. Besides, I tried to call her again when I left to tell her what happened, but she didn't answer."

Harrison showed the officers another time stamp on his phone, which registered three minutes after the alarm sounded. While he needed Victoria to answer his first call, he prayed she didn't answer his second. Harrison disconnected in relief when her voice message triggered. It proved to be another strategic undertaking hatched as part of the master plan. He wasn't sure what he would have said if she answered the second call, especially during that specific fearful time.

The officers examined the mobile phone for the second outgoing call to the same number. It checked out.

Harrison paused for the officers, then continued, "She knew the alarm would sound when she gave me the old code. She suggested I leave when it sounded to make it look like I left the *scene of the crime*, as you suggested. I went inside and checked the thermostat. I didn't think I was a threat since I was there to help."

Harrison could see that the officers were buying his story. He rehearsed the conversation multiple times last night as he laid awake.

He went on, "Did she hesitate when she told you it was me on the grainy video? Probably not, right?"

Harrison remained calm and awaited their response. That Persuasive Communication class at Butler was coming in handy now. Harrison was almost enjoying the conversation with the officers. He only hoped he wasn't smiling as he was slowly turning the blame on Victoria.

"Ok. You seem to be telling us the truth. I'll write this up once I get back to the station, but you may need to explain yourself at least one more time. In the meantime, stay away from the property."

"Fair enough. Thanks, officers."

Harrison ushered Claire back inside the house. She was still in shock over what happened and how her husband handled the situation.

"Did you just outsmart Victoria Marks?" she asked.

Harrison smiled. "It's easy to play the game as long as you know the rules."

Claire knew that about her husband. It was no surprise. He was a strategic and quick thinker. She wasn't sure if she should be mad at him or hug him.

Harrison figured he should call their attorney. It was best to tell Molly Eckles the story instead of hearing it from someone else. Besides, she would be able to keep the wolves at bay and maybe even find a little humor.

Most importantly, Harrison had the ring.

TWENTY-SIX

"My mouth speaks what is true, for my lips detest wickedness."

HARRISON AND CLAIRE DREADED THE DAY BUT THERE WAS NO WAY around it. The judge required the deposition, and Molly Eckles was happy to support the request.

Eckles saw this as an opportunity for the young Marks couple to share what they knew about Harlan's case. Molly understood that they had little knowledge, which played into her client's favor. Eckles was trying to tell the U.S. Assistant Attorney, David Costello, the entire time that her clients were innocent and had nothing to gain. She was adamant that if Harlan was not Harrison's father, then the younger Marks would not be pulled into this mess.

Molly coached both Harrison and Claire, but her clients were going to tell the truth, and if they didn't know the answer, they would share that as well.

Eckles pulled her clients aside one last time. "Remember what I said. You have three answers. 'Yes', 'no' and 'I don't know.'"

"Seems easy enough," Harrison sighed.

Costello and FBI Special Agent Spawn met the three in the lobby of the downtown government building. A court reporter joined them to capture the conversation in full detail.

"Well, I guess I'm supposed to do a little spiel just for the record," Costello stumbled.

He mentioned those present in the room and offered their titles before he got to Harrison and Claire.

He reminded the group why they were present.

"We are here today in the matter of the United States vs. Harlan Marks, particularly concerning the forfeiture of the case. Present to be deposed are Harrison Marks and Claire Marks, and both are represented by their attorney, Molly Eckles."

He gave more background stating, "The Marks claim their home property is not subject to forfeiture because they are bona fide purchasers of the residence."

He continued, "At the time the couple bought the property from their father, the Defendant in this case, they had no reason to believe that the property was subject to forfeiture."

Harrison nodded his head approvingly.

"They are here today because we served a notice of deposition. We also served them a subpoena for various financial records that relate to the petitions they filed and the motions for summary judgment, which they filed."

Costello wrapped it up. "Do you have anything to add, Ms. Eckles?"

Molly perked up. "Nothing," she said as she flipped Costello the middle finger under the table – only for Harrison to see.

He did a double-take and smirked inconspicuously at his councilor.

Costello told the Marks that some questions may be uncomfortable but to answer them to the best of their knowledge. His first question took the young couple by surprise.

"Have either of you ever participated in anything like this before,?" Costello asked. Both Harrison and Claire looked at him like he was an idiot.

"I will need you to answer all questions orally rather than by nodding or shaking your head since we are recording the conversation on manuscript. So, please state your answer to the question."

"No," both stated, raising their voice while also confirming that they did think he was an idiot.

"Also, don't worry if you need a break. Time is not an issue. If you need to speak to Ms. Eckles before you answer a question or confer with her in private, please ask."

The cross-examination began. Costello focused most of his time with Harrison.

Questions focused on his past work experience and job functions, and Harrison answered each one. Costello was building to Harrison's work experience at Marks Medical Supply.

The line of questioning included everything from earnings, job function, time spent in meetings with his father, interaction with others, and products that came in and out of the medical supply business.

Costello seemed disappointed in Harrison's answers. Andrew Spawn was upset with his answers.

Molly Eckles was right. Both men were hoping for nuggets of information that would help build their case against Harlan Marks. Everyone knew the meeting was about the house – even though the property's contract had already been provided to the Assistant U.S. Attorney in black and white.

Costello then asked about where Harrison went to college and how he paid for it. This was all a waste of time since Harrison's mom worked for the university and, therefore, his tuition was free.

"Did you receive any academic honors?" Costello asked.

"Yes."

"What honors did you receive?" Costello pressed.

"Is any of this relevant?" Harrison snapped. "Is this what the good tax-payers who pay your salary want to know?"

"Let's take a break," Eckles quickly suggested to Costello.

The parties broke up, and Molly Eckles walked to an empty conference room with the Marks following behind. Harrison was agitated, and Claire and Eckles were agitated with Harrison.

"Don't let him get to you," Eckles scolded. "These are easy questions. Answer them honestly – that's it. We are proving we have nothing to hide, and he looks like a fool. When the judge sees the recorded manuscript, he's going to recognize it was a waste of time. In the meantime, we need to cooperate."

They returned to the meeting room. Harrison felt like he had just been to the principal's office, so he took his seat like a good student with a fake smile on his face.

"Ready to continue?" Costello asked.

Additional mindless questions followed, and Harrison answered each one without further outbursts, but not without sarcasm.

"One of the unfortunate responsibilities I have in this job is to ask people about their relationships, and I hope you understand it's necessary," Costello stated. "I want to talk about your relationship with your father and Victoria."

Costello looked at Harrison waiting for an answer, but Harrison didn't respond because he didn't ask a question.

"Would you describe the two of you as having a close, father/son relationship?"

"No."

"How would you describe it then?"

"We saw each other on obligatory holidays and birthdays," Harrison responded.

"By your choice or his?"

"His."

"And what about Victoria?"

"I don't understand the question," Harrison challenged.

"What is your relationship with Victoria Marks."

"She's my father's wife," Harrison stated. He was not willing to acknowledge that Victoria was his stepmother.

"Were you close with Victoria?"

"No."

"Why is that?"

"She and my dad were always together. If I didn't see him, I didn't see her."

Costello moved away from Harrison's relationship with his father and Victoria and began to focus on sources of income.

He inquired about cash gifts that Harlan and Victoria provided to the young couple to help purchase the house and property.

Harrison breezed through those questions and shared that cash did not exchange hands.

Costello pushed the issue, but Eckles spoke up, "Objection. The Assistant U.S. Attorney has already been provided this information in detail."

Costello moved on, but he continued to find out if other sources of income helped support the young couple.

"Did anybody, unfortunately, pass away and leave you any money in the last five years?"

"Unfortunately, no," Harrison quipped.

Costello found the humor. "I suppose it depends on your perspective," as he smiled back.

More questions followed regarding credit card balances, stock holdings, and savings accounts.

Finally, Costello asked questions regarding the property and house.

Costello and Spawn were very interested in how Harrison and Claire could pay for a house valued at $425,000 over 30 years. They also wanted to know why the first note of $200,000 was due in-full to his father five years after the original execution of the contract.

"We entered the agreement with the understanding that Claire and I would refinance the value of the entire house with a lending institution."

"And did you refinance?

"Yes."

"I see you refinanced a total of $325,000, but the value of the home was $425,000. Is it true you paid $15,000 to your father as a down payment?"

"Yes."

"Is it also true that the agreement required you to provide payments to your father totaling approximately $35,000 to-date?"

"Yes."

"So you have already paid approximately $50,000 toward the property and refinanced for $325,000?

How many times do I have to answer this question, Harrison thought?

"Yes."

"Is it true that as part of the refinancing package, your father gifted you $50,000 to make up the difference in value?"

"Objection. This is outside the timeline and the scope of discovery. It has no bearing on whether they purchased for value and no bearing on whether they had legal rights or a title in the property. I'm instructing my clients not to answer," Eckles stated.

After much debate between Eckles and Costello, they both agreed to contact the judge to weigh in on the line of questioning.

The judge agreed with Costello. "This seems to address whether or not it will lead to discoverable or admissible evidence and appropriate examination. This may not be admissible evidence, but it's within the scope of cross-examination. The question could be subject to a motion filed by Ms. Eckles later. For now, your client will need to answer the question."

Molly Eckles felt better about the fact that she could later file a motion to make the questioning inadmissible. She agreed with the judge to proceed, although she didn't have a choice.

Costello continued. "So, the $50,000 was the difference between what you could afford to finance and your total payoff on the original loans that you had with your father and Victoria Marks? Is that correct?"

"Yes."

"Therefore, the $50,000 was an outright gift with no repayment expected?"

"Yes."

That's what they were after all along. The government wanted to know how much money Harlan and Victoria gifted to the younger Marks. Harrison realized their tactics were to reclaim a $50,000 monetary gift. Although no actual money exchanged hands, Harlan and Victoria forgave the difference between the total value of the house and what was already paid.

Costello and Spawn thought they knew what was owed, but these statements would help solidify their case. Once the number was established and through recorded deposition, the government could begin to put a price tag on the debt owed on Harrison and Claire's behalf. They argued that any monetary gift provided by Harlan Marks should rightfully be the property of the government.

An hour later, the deposition ended with Costello confirming and re-confirming the financial gift amount that never exchanged hands.

This could have been addressed from the beginning, but Harrison and Claire were convinced they purchased the property free and clear from his father. They could have agreed to pay any amount upfront depending upon what the government deemed reasonable. However, they knew they needed to fight to salvage their nest egg. Now they both knew it was time to come to an agreement – fighting any longer would mean more attorney expenses and stress. Cutting losses would also get them out from under the property lien.

"Get with Costello and come up with a settlement," Harrison instructed Eckles as the elevator door closed. "It's time to move on."

Molly Eckles understood.

TWENTY-SEVEN

"A gentle answer turns away wrath,
but a harsh word stirs up anger."

THE WEEKS PASSED QUICKLY. COLD WINTER DAYS WERE REPLACED BY signs of spring and a newborn baby that demanded attention.

Harrison took a three-week break from visiting his father to appease Claire and spend a few weekends with his family. It was nice to sleep in an extra day if Becca would allow it. Anyway, he was furious with his father after the house incident.

But Harrison continued to find himself dreading another Sunday morning visit to the downtown jail. By this time, Mimi nearly demanded to see her son. She was not about to allow a fourth weekend to go by without a fight.

Mimi disregarded the fact Harrison had a wife, a baby, and a job with daily demands. It never crossed her mind her grandson may want to spend his weekends focused on something other than Harlan.

For her, it was the highlight of her week. Before, Harlan called his mother every night. She talked while he tried to listen. Now it was different. He was allowed one phone call per week, and he used the opportunity to call Victoria.

Harrison called Mimi the night before to plan for the visit. He wasn't sure why. They already discussed the arrangements earlier that week, but he was certain Mimi appreciated the call.

The two made the trip the next morning and followed the same route downtown. As usual, they arrived just in time to be two of the last people to make the visitation list.

As they sat down with Harlan, Mimi asked the usual questions. Harrison waited as he had a lot on his mind. He needed some answers from his father.

"Your wife tried to have me arrested."

"Oh, no, Harrison. It's just that she's been so scared. Unfortunately, I wasn't able to talk to her before you went to the house. She didn't know what was happening, and she panicked. It was just a misunderstanding."

"Bullshit. I'm done doing anything to help."

Harrison said his peace and didn't pursue the argument any further. Besides, he got his point across.

Harrison settled when he heard his father speak. "It sounds like the judge is preparing to make a final decision on the length of my sentence and where I'll be doing my time."

He paused for his son to respond, but Harrison remained silent.

His father continued, "Hausmann also said it might help if family members wrote a letter to the judge before sentencing. He thinks it's worth a shot to help minimize the time on my sentence."

"I thought you already made a plea deal," Harrison asked.

"I'm doing everything I can to keep the sentence down. Regardless, Hausmann is arranging for me to do my time in Morgantown, WV. It's a prison for people that committed white-collar crimes. I understand it's a little more laid back than other prisons where they keep inmates who are killers and rapists."

"So, what are you asking?"

"Well, I want the two of you, and anyone willing, to write a letter asking the judge to reduce the sentence before he makes his final judgment. Tell him I'm a good person, father, and son. Is that something you're willing to do?"

"We can do that," Mimi stated willingly.

Harrison turned and looked at his grandmother, who took it upon herself to volunteer them both.

"I need these letters submitted to my attorney by the end of the week."

That's not much time, Harrison thought to himself.

The guard announced the visitation was over. The visitors shuffled to the elevator.

"The letters!" Harlan announced as the elevator door began to shut.

"Yes. The letters," Harrison mumbled to himself.

Mimi reminded Harrison on the ride home to send the letters and asked how he would ensure the letters arrived on time to Hausmann.

"Email me your letter by Wednesday night," he said, knowing the old woman didn't even a computer or a cell phone.

Once again, his remark didn't sit well with her.

"This is something your father needs from us."

"Yes, and let's make sure we make this a priority and do everything in our power to make this happen," Harrison said sarcastically.

"Yes," she agreed, not picking up on her grandson's satire.

Harrison returned home to Claire. He shared the events of the morning and then announced his father's request.

"He wants us to write letters to help him? Where was his help when we needed him to make us a part of the plea deal?" Claire questioned. "I'll be damned if I'm writing a letter to benefit him. I've considered writing a letter to him outlining what I think of him and reminding him of what he has done to you and his elderly mother."

"I don't have an issue with you writing him a letter," Harrison mentioned.

For a long time, Harrison had taken a few shots from Claire about his father. She knew the current circumstance wasn't Harrison's fault, but someone had to hear what she had to say, and Harrison took it personally.

She knew her husband spent too much time being the devoted son to a father only concerned about himself. Claire also knew it was time for

Harrison to be emotionally present with her and Becca. His father still consumed him.

"Are you going to write a letter for him?" Claire asked.

"Not sure. I don't think it's going to help."

"Is that the only reason you wouldn't write it?"

"Not sure," was the response again, trying to avoid further confrontation.

Later that week, Harrison went to his grandmother's apartment to get her letter and letters from distant family members.

He decided he wasn't writing a letter on his father's behalf, but he was happy to help Mimi.

"Have you written your letter yet?" she asked.

"No."

That evening, his phone rang. It was a collect call from the jail.

"You are receiving a collect call from Harlan Marks at the Marion County Jail. Do you wish to accept the charges?"

"Yes."

Harlan jumped right in, "Hey, how are you doing?"

"I'm fine. How are you?"

"I have a question for you. I spoke with my attorney today. You haven't dropped off any letters to his office. Are you still planning to bring them?"

"Yes. Why?"

"Well, I wasn't sure. It's just that things I've been asking of you don't seem to be taken seriously," Harlan suggested.

At that moment, Harrison became someone he didn't know. He experienced a jolt of electricity course through his body as if he was on fire. He began to shake, and he became speechless. A switch flipped inside him – he had enough.

All his life, Harrison was submissive to his father. Regardless of their disagreements, Harrison always found his way back to his dad to make amends.

Now years of anger devoured him, and the selfishness his father displayed for the past few years was too much. The fact that his father wasn't invested emotionally in his family disturbed him. Harrison felt overwhelming resentment because he never stood up to his father.

Harrison was full of outrage and everything became clear. He was about to stand on his own and say everything to release the chains weighing him down.

"Are you kidding me?" Harrison shouted into the phone.

He didn't let his father answer.

"I have done everything you asked me to do and more. I'm the only one holding it all together for your family, including your elderly mother. You have destroyed her after everything she's given you."

Harrison let that sink in for a moment.

"By the way, your bitch of a wife doesn't do a damn thing to support your ass. You're doing everything in your power to make sure she gets through this unscathed and with no prison time. Are you having the same conversation with her?"

"What have you done for me, your only child? You know, the father to your only grandchild! What have you done to get me out of this mess? Not a damn thing. You left me hanging."

"You…," his father tried to interject.

Harrison didn't allow it. The younger Marks was feeling empowered with emotion that had built up for too long. He was angry yet controlled and confident with his words.

"Even more, you pretend like you're innocent. You think you're always the smartest person in the room. Well, you're not. You can't even admit when you've done wrong."

By this point, Claire overheard her husband's booming voice from the other end of the house, and she now stood in the office doorway.

"You know what you are?" Harrison asked pointedly. "You're a damn coward. Only a coward could act this way."

Harrison struck a nerve with his prideful father. He likely struck many nerves and now silenced himself to see how his father would respond.

Harlan was put back on his heels. His son had never spoken to him this way, and he wasn't prepared.

Harlan stammered, "A coward? Let me tell you something. I'm not a coward. I'm a man. I'm a man that..."

Harrison laughed and didn't hesitate to interrupt the older Marks.

"A man?" he asked sarcastically. Harrison's voice remained loud, forceful, and intimidating.

"You're no man," Harrison mocked. "A real man doesn't desert his family. A real man doesn't try to show off his possessions. A real man doesn't steal from others, and a real man sure as hell doesn't run from the law. You're nothing but a coward."

"And don't expect a letter from me," Harrison added before ending the call.

Claire stood silently, giving him a moment to compose himself. She knew this was a difficult moment for Harrison, but also one that needed to happen. Her husband needed to break away from his father's emotional grasp to take his first step toward healing. This outburst was part of the process. She realized there was nothing she needed to say. She knew it would be another sleepless night for her husband.

Harrison gathered the letters and placed them in his backpack to drop off at Jason Hausmann's office on his way through town tomorrow morning. They weren't going to make a difference, but Harrison didn't care. His father deserved whatever sentence he received.

The three letters intended for the judge didn't include one significant letter.

Shortly after Harrison ended the call with his father, Claire sat down and composed a letter intended directly for her father-in-law.

It was her turn to share how she felt. Harlan felt the wrath of his son. Now he was about to hear from Claire. She dropped it in the mail the next day.

The weekend came along, and Harrison received the usual call from his grandmother. She was unhappy and hurt when he told her he would no longer be going to the jail on Sunday mornings.

"I'm really sorry, but I can no longer support him," Harrison said.

"Well, can you at least take me?" Mimi asked.

"I'm sorry. I can't do it. I have spent too much time away from Claire and Becca."

"You're a terrible grandson for doing this to me. Even more, you're a terrible son. I can't believe you would do this to him," Mimi repeated.

Harrison raised his voice only to be firm. "I didn't do this to him. He did this to himself."

He composed himself so he wouldn't say anything regretful.

"Besides, I've taken you downtown countless times. You have a car, and you still drive. There isn't anyone on the roads that early on Sunday mornings."

"I don't pay attention to the way we go," she stated.

Harrison knew she wasn't telling the truth. Mimi knew her way downtown. Harrison didn't care; he only knew he wasn't going.

"You have friends. You can have one of them take you."

Mimi hung up without another word. The old lady was very angry with her grandson.

It didn't matter. Harrison had to focus on his family.

TWENTY-EIGHT

"In all your ways acknowledge Him,
and he will make your paths straight."

HARRISON AND CLAIRE SECURED A SEPARATE LOAN TO PAY THE IRS. The deal included the couple paying the government $50,000, the full amount that Harlan and Victoria gifted. Harrison didn't see any sense in spending more money on a defense attorney when it became clear the judge would not side with the young couple.

Both parties signed the papers, and the Marks were now the rightful owners of the property and home, according to the IRS.

Harrison thought the birth of their daughter and clearing their name with the government would change his perspective, and it did for a short time. However, it didn't take long before he eventually drifted backward. Even with the birth of Becca, Harrison's mind was never present in the moment. Anger, resentment, and bitterness toward his father consumed his thoughts.

His father's verdict came down from the Federal District Court in late spring.

The judge granted Harlan's request to transfer to Morgantown, West Virginia. The transfer meant Harrison didn't have to feel pressured to take his grandmother for visits. She wouldn't expect him to drive from Indianapolis to Morgantown each month. It was selfish on his part, but Harrison found it was the best way for him to move on.

Once the verdict was handed down, the media frenzy picked up again. What had died down since last September was now back on the front page of every newspaper, television station, and social media page in Indiana and beyond.

There was nowhere for Harrison and Claire to escape.

Harlan Marks was indicted originally on various charges of Medicare fraud and money laundering. The government accepted his guilty plea after Harlan withdrew his previous plea – *not guilty*.

At the time of the indictment, the government granted a preliminary order of forfeiture, which authorized them to seize the properties in question. As part of the deal, Harlan waived the notice and the right to appeal the order of forfeiture. He would no longer fight for control of the real estate.

The property seized by the government included all the property owned by Marks Management Services, Inc., an Indiana Corporation wholly owned by Harlan and Victoria Marks.

Third-party lenders who held mortgages on the real estate petitioned the district court for hearings to settle the validity of the legal interests. Multiple lenders filed petitions asserting they had valid, priority liens on specific properties. If they weren't going to get paid, they felt they rightfully owned the property.

Highlighted in the ruling, the government determined that Harlan and Victoria Marks amassed a real estate empire consisting of several residential rental properties in Indianapolis. According to the government, each property was financed by defrauding the federal Medicare program.

During the three-year period when Medicare first paid Marks Medical Supply for fraudulent claims and when the government acted against Harlan, the government claimed that Harlan used over $8 million of the fraudulent money as a down payment for dozens of properties worth at least $25 million.

Harrison knew those numbers were low. Benton Jeffers, Harlan and Victoria's personal attorney, told Harrison that his father received Medicare payments of more than $15.5 million, and the forfeited properties were valued at well over $40 million. Even more, Harlan and Marks Medical Supply submitted an additional $26.7 million that was waiting for Medicare approval.

Two years ago, federal agents caught on to Harlan and executed the search warrants to secure documents at the offices of Marks Medical Supply, the company used to defraud Medicare, and at Marks Management Service, Inc., the company Harlan used to manage his rental properties.

The government also stated that within three months after the documents were seized, Harlan established a shell corporation called Ashton Button Company, Ltd. in the Cayman Islands, and a second shell corporation called Iguana Reef, Ltd., also in the Cayman Islands. The elder Marks established them as a loophole to hide offshore riches and maintain anonymity.

It became obvious that Harlan and Victoria Marks were planning to flee the country when they began to close bank accounts and sell real estate once they realized they were not going to win the case against the government. Harlan was not inconspicuous about converting many holdings into liquid assets.

Over 18 months, Harlan wire-transferred at least $2.7 million to the Cayman Islands. He used these funds to buy real estate in the name of his two Cayman Island corporations. The government alleged that he obtained the funds wired to the Cayman Islands from several sources. The IRS also knew most of the funds came from the refinancing of the apartment buildings.

There was further evidence that Harlan purchased a waterfront residence in the Cayman Islands valued at $600,000 just before his arrest, along with additional undeveloped land valued at $2.5 million.

Harlan Mark's reign as the real estate mogul of Indianapolis came to an end. Harlan was sentenced to 70 months in federal prison.

As expected, Victoria remained an unindicted co-conspirator and did not serve prison time.

As much as Harrison thought he was prepared for the final verdict, the verdict was difficult to digest.

It was a harsh reality to know life would never be the same. Everyone he knew in high school, college, and business would forever link him to his father. Old friends no longer knew what to say to him. Conversations never went further than shallow, courteous exchanges.

The neighbors didn't know how to respond. As summer came, Harrison and Claire avoided neighborhood parties and boat gatherings at the sandbar. They wanted to save everyone from the awkward discussion. Besides, the Marks felt like they would be interrupting the gossip, knowing they were the likely topic.

Harrison's discontent for his father grew. It already brought disgrace upon the family, sadness for his grandmother, a significant financial penalty to him and Claire, and a wedge that seemed insurmountable between him and his father.

His father's decisions affected every relationship, family or not, although they were becoming accustomed to isolation. They used Becca as an excuse, but Harrison's isolation went deeper.

Claire managed well on the surface. She was intent on being a good mother, and her thoughts were always on Becca. Even after she went back to work, the mention of Becca's name easily put a smile on her face.

Claire's biggest challenge was dropping her daughter off at a babysitter each morning. Those moments were difficult.

She always considered herself a career woman, but now she began to question her purpose. She loved her career, and she was rewarded handsomely with the human resource manager title and a hefty salary to back it up. She was proud of what she accomplished, but now she had Becca to consider.

Harrison knew what Claire was going through, and he wanted to ease her burden. His effort to make life easier for her only fueled his anger and resentment toward his father. The more he isolated himself, the more time he spent on the circumstances.

Claire and Harrison were different in this capacity. Claire threw herself into being a mother to her daughter – being a mom helped her avoid dealing with other issues.

Harrison was the opposite. He wanted to handle his problems directly and on his own until he found a solution.

Both strategies were a defense mechanism, and both strategies were failing.

In Claire's defense, she was spending a lot of quality time with Becca. Claire was an outstanding mother and interacted with her daughter through nursing, trips to the store, playtime, boat rides, walks, baths, and even naps.

Harrison admired their relationship, especially since he had trouble connecting with his daughter. Whenever Harrison held Becca, she cried. She was picking up on her father's anxiety. It wouldn't take long before Harrison handed his daughter back to Claire. Claire was sweet to suggest that she spoiled their daughter, and that's why Becca wanted her mom. However, Harrison became discouraged and isolated himself even more.

He started to have nightmares that caused him to wake up soaked in sweat. During these night terrors, Agent Spawn would break into his home and kidnap Becca from her crib while Harrison was locked in his bedroom, unable to save his daughter.

After two weeks of this horror, Harrison tucked Becca in her infant carrier and placed her next to his side of the bed for peace of mind. Claire didn't challenge her husband, even though she didn't understand.

Harrison became distracted and couldn't focus on the important tasks. He missed valuable time with his wife and daughter because he was focused on the troubles his father caused. He couldn't let go and became angry at himself.

How did I not see this coming? He couldn't stop blaming himself.

He thought back to when his dad offered to sell the house. Harrison should have said no, but he was captivated by the property's beauty.

Why did he think the search warrants at Marks Medical Supply would go away and never be heard about again?

I believed everything that he told me, Harrison thought to himself.

Harrison was angry that he never challenged his father and didn't investigate more on his own. Was he naïve or careless? Regardless, it cost him dearly.

He wondered if it would have mattered if they didn't purchase the house. He wouldn't be affected financially, but he would still have to contend with the drama.

Regardless, he was upset that he couldn't fix his wife's pain. Harlan wasn't her father, and she didn't deserve this predicament. It was Harrison's job to protect his wife, and he couldn't do it. He couldn't even protect her from his own family. The damage was done, and Harrison wasn't sure how to help himself or his wife recover. Harrison felt guilt and shame, not just because of the bad choices that his father made, but because he was unable to shield himself and Claire.

He wasn't prepared to forgive himself, let alone his father.

The situation burdened him endlessly. He searched for an answer from someone other than himself. God wasn't answering. Harrison felt empty and lonely.

He went through the motions each day, trusting that Claire was taking care of everything, including Becca.

His father's case had been over for four months. Harlan was in Morgantown, and the media blitz had settled. A couple of times a week, he talked to his grandmother. The conversations were difficult but manageable.

Harrison should have moved on with his new family, but he still wasn't whole. Harrison needed to get his mentally ravaged life back on track. He wasn't experiencing the full joy of being a husband or a dad.

Summer turned to fall, and Claire and Harrison sat on the bed together one evening. Little Becca was situated between them, and Zoe was finally settled at the bottom of the bed submerged under the covers.

Harrison waited all day for this moment. There was something on his mind.

"This isn't working, Claire."

"What are you talking about?"

"The fact that we're taking Becca to daycare every day. We're not getting to spend quality time with her. We get her ready in the morning, and we don't see her all day. Then, we bring her home in the early evening just in time to feed her, bathe her, and get her to bed. We don't spend enough time with her. We're missing out."

Claire agreed with Harrison's recap of their daughter's weekly schedule. However, she also knew Harrison had missed opportunities with Becca.

"So, what are you saying?"

"I had a meeting today with my managers and floated the idea of me managing my sales territory from Madison, Indiana."

He had Claire's full attention.

"They felt I could be more valuable to the company if I lived there because we currently don't have anyone covering that part of the state or getting into Louisville. They said to let them know if I was serious. They even offered to pay for the move since it would benefit them."

Claire was shocked. Although the couple had talked about selling the house and moving to Madison since they paid the government, Claire didn't take the conversation seriously until now. She was processing the possibility.

"You've mentioned that you would like to stay home to raise Becca. We can afford to live off my income if we move to Madison. We can't do that in Indy. If we stay here, you will have to continue to work, and we'll have to continue to take Becca to daycare."

It was true; Claire wanted more time with Becca. She was nearly a year old and growing fast. The little girl was close to taking her first steps, and Claire knew that she might not be around to see it. She didn't want to miss other milestones.

"I'll have to quit my job," Claire realized.

"Yes. It will be a difficult commute otherwise," Harrison mocked, trying to get her to smile.

"Think about it. You can see your parents whenever you want while raising our daughter at home."

That was appealing to Claire, who was very close with her mother. They talked on the phone every other night.

"Maybe we could even start attending church," Harrison added as the final kicker.

He understood this was something Claire wanted, but most importantly, she wanted Becca to grow up with a strong church family and youth program.

Harrison also knew the only time he and Claire attended service was when they visited her parents once a month in Madison. He found comfort in the music and Pastor Bob's sermons.

"It's the life we've always talked about, Claire. It's what you've always wanted – this is our opportunity."

Claire smiled another perfect smile.

"It's a new start with people who don't know our story," she added in a sigh of relief.

Two days later, the Marks placed a real estate sign in the front yard.

TWENTY-NINE

"The heart of the discerning acquires knowledge,
for the ears of the wise seek it out."

THE HOUSE SOLD QUICKLY – TWO WEEKS TO BE EXACT.
Harrison's mom was shocked to hear that her only son was moving far away, and his house sold so soon.

Mimi took it hard when she found out as well. For months, Harrison and Claire made a point to bring her to the house for weekend meals and spend time with her great-granddaughter. She tried to understand why they were moving. Now, at 91 years old, she was going to be without her son and her grandson.

It was also a sad day when Claire gave her employer notice. She loved her job, and she knew she would likely not see the people again, although she told herself otherwise. Her colleagues organized an emotional going-away party for her on her last day.

Her parents, on the other hand, were elated with the news. They never thought they would see the day that their daughter moved back to the small town of fewer than 13,000 people.

The Marks settled nicely in the new community after only a few months. They rented a townhouse while they searched to purchase a new home. The couple decided to build when they found a perfect lot on the northwest corner of town. They would break ground the following spring and move into their custom home in the fall.

Madison was a tight community. The school system was strong, and most of the teachers lived in the community. Many of them were graduates of Madison who went away to college and returned home to teach.

Most importantly, Claire knew the people when she ventured to the grocery store, post office, or when she and Harrison went to dinner while leaving Becca with Maw Maw and Paw Paw. She felt at ease, and Harrison noticed how much she enjoyed being a stay-at-home mom.

Harrison enjoyed church and looked forward to Pastor Bob's sermons each Sunday. He was surprised to learn church was as much about the community gathering as it was celebrating God. Everyone seemed to attend each Sunday morning.

It was coming together for Harrison, but not entirely as he had hoped. He still held on to the demons he tried to leave behind in Indianapolis. The resentment toward his father festered. It was a constant reminder of his permanent and emotional scars. The same scars were likely visible to anyone else who spent time with him. He was able to meet people but felt the need to protect himself against forging deep relationships.

He knew that if he revealed why he moved his family from Indianapolis to Madison it could be damning in the small town where news travels fast. He would be humiliated if the people of Madison learned his real identity.

Old habits being hard to break, the couple gathered in the bedroom to wind down for the evening. Zoe burrowed deep beneath the covers.

Until now, Claire gave her husband a lot of time to adjust to small-town living.

"So, how do you like living in Madison?" she finally asked.

Harrison looked at her and thought for a moment.

"It's not much different than Indy."

She was surprised by his answer as this was not how she intended to steer the conversation.

"Really?

"Well, once Claire was born, we stayed home most of the time. We do the same thing here, just in a different town," Harrison explained.

Claire pondered his response, and she knew her husband was right. The Marks lifestyle was about the same – it was only the location that changed.

"So, do you like it here?" she asked, hoping she would get the answer she was seeking.

"Yes, I'm happy. You get to live closer to your parents and stay home to raise Becca. We have a good school, and we have a church to meet new people and worship."

Harrison knew that Claire was meeting other stay-at-home moms at church. The ladies often invited her and Becca to join them for playdates and story time at the library. Friday night drinks also were part of the equation once a month but only for the moms.

She was developing needed friendships, and it made Harrison happy.

Claire, however, was still concerned for her husband. Harrison continued to wrestle with the anger he had toward his father.

"I just hope no one here finds out about my dad," her husband said right on queue. The conversation she intended was back on course.

"We'll deal with it when necessary," she stated. "Are you ready to talk to Pastor Bob yet? I mentioned it about a year ago."

"Why do I need to talk to him?"

"Well, you're concerned with how others are going to respond if they find out about his past…our past," she corrected herself. "But how do you expect to respond if *you* haven't dealt with it?"

"I don't know," Harrison replied quietly.

Claire noticed that Harrison started to withdrawal from the conversation. She left him with one final thought.

"If you want to find joy, you need to address it."

Harrison knew Claire was right. While he was happy for Claire's fresh start in Madison, he couldn't experience the same joy. He was happy, but withdrew when something reminded him of his father. These moments happened often, and it continued to steal time away from his family.

It took another two months for Harrison to take his first step. Christmas past and now into January, the sermon series focused on *forgiveness*.

Harrison didn't think much of it until he was handed the bulletin and walked into the sanctuary. The title of the first sermon, *Forgiving God*, caught him off guard.

"When we think of forgiveness," Pastor Bob started, "We think of forgiving others. I begin by saying that life is fundamentally about two relationships. First is our relationship with God, and second is our relationship with other people. These relationships are the essential ingredients for life. Relationships, however, are not always smooth. Meaningful relationships require tweaks and sometimes major adjustments along the way if we want them to last. The reason so many relationships fail is that one or both individuals aren't willing to take these steps."

Harrison listened intently. It wasn't unusual that Pastor Bob's sermon's resonated with the congregation, but this was about to strike a nerve.

Pastor Bob continued, "I want to focus on the primary relationship in our life. I chose to title my sermon today, *Forgiving God*. Now you could read this two ways. Most of you probably looked at the title and thought you need to forgive God for things he allowed to happen to you in your life. That's not a surprise. It could also mean that we have a God that is forgiving. I want to touch on both as they may be related."

The hair stood up on the back of Harrison's neck, and he felt his body go numb. He considered himself the only person in the room, and Pastor Bob was speaking directly to him.

The pastor continued and reminded the congregation that our Christian belief affirms God is perfect and has never done anything wrong. He then suggested God has never needed forgiveness.

Harrison wasn't in agreement with the last comment. He believed that both individuals must work hard to make a relationship work.

He refocused on the sermon just in time to hear Pastor Bob say, "If we are honest with ourselves, we admit that we have felt as if God messed something up in our lives. Maybe he didn't intervene at the right time, or maybe he didn't intervene at all."

Yes, Harrison confirmed silently.

"Maybe you even think God owes you an apology. Sometimes terrible things happen that make us question God. Why did he let this happen?"

Even though Harrison knew deep down that God doesn't make mistakes, he still held a grudge. The grudge wasn't just against his father; it was also against God.

Harrison was about to detach from the sermon. He wasn't prepared for how hard the words hit his heart.

Pastor Bob brought him back. "Did you know that if you have been mad at God, you might be in good company? The Bible illustrates several significant people of faith have expressed frustration, resentment, and anger at God."

Moses, King David, Job, and Jonah were a few of the names the pastor mentioned. These were all names Harrison recognized from his childhood Sunday School classes. At the time, he interpreted them only as cartoon characters of the Bible, and not real people of faith.

"So, is it ok to be mad at God?" the pastor asked. "Well, there's a difference between sharing your most gut-wrenching emotions with God and believing God is the cause for those emotions. Perhaps it's best described in the following verse.

Pastor Bob called attention to Psalm 22 where David states, *"My God, my God, why have you forsaken me? Why are you so far from saving me, so far from my cries of anguish? My God, I cry out by day, but you do not answer, by night, but I find no rest."*

Harrison heard the scripture. The spoken words cried out with frustration and honesty. He understood David's words of abandonment during his moment of need.

The scripture continued, *"Yet you are enthroned as the Holy One; you are the one Israel praises. In you our ancestors put their trust; they trusted and you delivered them. To you they cried out and were saved; in you, they trusted and were not put to shame."*

Harrison disengaged from the sermon once again.

It was evident that even during David's distress and anger, he still had faith. David knew that God had shown up in the past and that God would show up again.

Harrison concluded that God didn't need his forgiveness – God needed his trust.

By the time Harrison snapped back to reality, the sermon was winding down. His head filled with thoughts. As a result, he missed a good portion of the sermon.

"I need to talk with Pastor Bob," Harrison said to Claire once everyone was dismissed.

Claire found her group of moms after church, and Harrison waited for Pastor Bob to finish shaking hands and saying goodbye to the congregation.

The Pastor noticed Harrison sitting in the pew and came over to greet him.

"Harrison, it's time to go home," he joked. "Most people are rushing to get out, but here you sit."

Harrison smiled, "I'm hoping you might have some time to talk."

"Sure. What's on your mind?"

"I'm guessing you know my story."

Pastor Bob nodded. He anticipated a day when Harrison might come forward.

"I'm sorry that happened," he acknowledged.

The two of them sat alone in the sanctuary.

"I've been angry with God. Then, I feel guilty about it. Am I allowed to be angry with God?"

"That's a great question that many people don't understand," Pastor Bob assured. "Let me ask you a question before I answer yours."

"Harrison, have you ever been angry with Claire as a result of an argument?"

Harrison looked around to find his wife, but it appeared she took the car and went home.

He laughed. "Sure."

"Do you love her?"

"Well, of course."

"Yes," the pastor reassured. "Of course, you love her."

"Harrison," he continued, "just because we love someone doesn't mean we can't be angry with them from time to time. That's a real relationship. God wants the *real* Harrison. Otherwise, it's not an authentic relationship," he added.

Harrison experienced a weight lifted from his shoulders.

"That's good to hear. I've been trying to suppress my anger at God. You know, make it go away."

"Many people try to make it go away when they're angry with God. Does your wife know when you are angry with her even when you don't tell her?" the pastor asked.

"Absolutely."

"Well, what makes you think God doesn't know?"

Harrison nodded, showing complete understanding.

"God knows your heart, Harrison. You might as well confess it to him. Trust me when I say that He is big enough to handle your anger and other frustrations or fears you give to Him.

Harrison smiled. "I suppose that's true."

"Yes, it's true. He's God. When you're mad at God, tell Him. He already knows anyway. That's the power of prayer – it's a direct link to Him. The worst response we can have when we are angry is to shut down communication. We must communicate everything with God, and we do that through prayer. Tell Him what you feel."

Emotions began to pour from Harrison. He choked back tears. "But He left us. He left Claire and me when we needed Him the most. We didn't deserve what happened to us. He didn't do anything to help."

"Really? Are you sure?"

Pastor Bob knew he had to peel back the many layers of Harrison's emphatic statement.

"Did you attend church when you lived in Indy?"

"No," Harrison said, wiping a tear.

"Did you talk with God when you lived in Indy?"

"Not really," Harrison said, wondering where he was going with the questions.

"Did you have friends there?"

"No."

"If you didn't go through the fire you just went through, would you still be living the same life you were living all along?"

"Probably."

"So, no church, no desire to have a real relationship with God, and no friends in your previous life," the pastor reminded him.

"Look where you are *right* now, Harrison. You're sitting with your pastor in church asking questions about God, wanting to know His greater plan for you. Here you have a loving congregation who, if you give them a chance, may become close friends to you and Claire."

He could see he was getting through to Harrison, and he continued.

"Claire now gets to stay at home and raise your daughter because you can afford to live on a single income. Would she have been able to do that in Indy?"

"No."

"Do you think this is all random, Harrison? Your new life didn't happen without God. If this misfortune never took place, you would still be living your life your way and not experiencing all that God intended for you and Claire. He never left you. He's been with you the entire time. You just didn't take the time to recognize it."

Pastor Bob was right. Harrison had no intentions of changing his life before this ordeal. He was very content doing things his way. Harrison also knew that he probably wouldn't have committed to a church. Until now, he never made it a priority. God never abandoned him. He abandoned God.

He allowed a moment for Harrison to catch up and then hit him again.

"Also, understand that God doesn't create our suffering, Harrison. But he does use these moments to sharpen us as Christians."

"What do you mean?"

"Well, typically in times of prosperity, we find ourselves pursuing the things of the world. But when we are truly suffering, the world is stripped away. It's in these moments that God has our full attention. He uses these moments to shape us into better followers of Christ. Often, it's not until we experience suffering that we swing our moral compass and begin chasing after God's heart."

"He's doing that to you right now. He's using your suffering to shape a new and improved Harrison Marks. I know that you felt as if your world was falling apart, but actually, God is using this as an opportunity to make your life everything He intended for you. Look around. Here you are. God is at work, Harrison."

The pastor quoted scripture from Psalm 23:4, *"Even though I walk through the valley of the shadow of death, I will fear no evil, for you are with me."*

Pastor Bob stopped short of finishing the verse and spoke to Harrison. "God doesn't promise us that we won't walk through valleys and dark times. He does promise us, if we follow Him, that He will always be in those valleys with us."

Harrison thanked the pastor and stood up. An hour had passed, and he walked outside to text Claire for a ride home.

He had a lot of information to consider, but he knew he wouldn't go through it alone. God was present, as He had been all along.

THIRTY

"Let your eyes look straight ahead,
fix your gaze directly before you."

A BIG PIECE OF THE PUZZLE FELL INTO PLACE FOR HARRISON. HE HAD a desire to seek a better understanding of God and what He wanted for him. Harrison realized that he was only living a life to get him through the day. He rose out of bed each morning, repeating the same mundane tasks as the day before.

Harrison was locked in the golden handcuffs. It was the routine that society says is necessary, acceptable, and safe. The golden handcuffs were easy because they provided stability without sacrifice. However, the handcuffs prevented him from the freedom that God intended.

Have a family, focus on your career, pay your bills, go on a vacation once a year, and have a few alcoholic drinks on the weekend to celebrate. By the way, make sure to mow the lawn, and take out the trash.

That was it. That was his life as he reflected on his time in Indianapolis.

After talking with Pastor Bob, Harrison had a different perspective. Until now, he overlooked the possibility that God had a plan designed specifically for Harrison Marks.

God wants so much more for me. No more blaming God, he thought.

Harrison still didn't understand the plan – that would take time. However, knowing God designed a blueprint and helped him begin that journey gave him peace.

That week he prayed each night and often during the day. It brought him comfort to share his heart with God. Prayer quieted his mind and brought him positive energy.

Harrison also found a few podcasts during his daily trips to visit customers who he was now happier to see.

Although he took a big step, it didn't solve all of his problems. He looked forward to the second week of the sermon series titled, *Forgiving Ourselves*.

Harrison wrestled with tremendous shame and embarrassment for the dishonor brought upon him. The people in his past looked at him differently. They saw a man with a family secret. Unfortunately, they were eager to tell others, but they were too uncomfortable to continue a relationship with the Marks.

It created many awkward moments while living in Indianapolis. Friends didn't know what to say and avoided talking to him. Neighbors waved from a distance but didn't go out of their way to offer support or condolences. People stayed clear of Harrison and Claire. Harrison understood because, under the same circumstances, he would have acted the same.

If people who already knew him pulled away, he was convinced anyone who discovered his past wouldn't want to be his friend. In doing so, they risked the same scorn. Who would want to socialize with someone who wore this *Scarlet Letter*?

Harrison even questioned if Claire would be interested in him if this happened before their marriage. Honestly, he was surprised she stayed with him. She didn't sign up for this, and he felt she deserved better. Did she feel stuck in this relationship?

At this point, all Harrison knew was that God was on his side.

Pastor Bob gave a great sermon, although it was emotional. Self-forgiveness, or in Harrison's case, shedding his armor of shame, seemed too great a task.

Again, he waited until the end of the church service to meet with his preacher.

"The sermon was tough for you, wasn't it, Harrison?" Pastor Bob asked, already knowing the answer.

"Yep."

Harrison shared his challenges.

"So why do you punish yourself?"

The young man was surprised by the question. He shared most of his hidden feelings – ones that he hadn't even revealed to Claire.

"I have these emotional scars that I wear every day," Harrison stated emphatically. "They have already turned away many of the people I know."

"Great analogy, Harrison. Let's talk about the scars you wear. They can serve one of two purposes. First, they bring shame and make us think we are ugly when we look at ourselves in the mirror. We convince ourselves that others see the same ugliness. Shame becomes a thief that tells us we don't measure up or don't belong. Sometimes we think people will mock us once we reveal our scars because they don't have the same scars. We see our scars, and we think they define us. We think that's the way others will define us."

Harrison agreed, and although it made him sad, he was glad the pastor understood.

"The other option is to allow those scars to be part of your story. In other words, your scars don't define you, but they do help shape you into the person God wants you to become.

Harrison was intrigued.

Pastor Bob shared an example, "Think about a man that walks with a permanent limp. When people ask him what happened to his leg, he shares his story. It's likely, the way he received his limp is the result of something painful."

Harrison understood as Pastor Bob continued.

"Here's the difference. Although the man is permanently affected by something very harmful, he now gives a voice to that permanent limp by sharing his story with others."

"Harrison, once you learn to accept your imperfections, then you can tell your story about how you received the emotional scars you describe. Then and only then, you'll experience the freedom you seek."

"But I need to talk about it?"

"Not necessarily in the sense that you have to stand up in front of a room full of people. However, you may find yourself in a situation with someone who needs to hear your example. Maybe this is how you share the Gospel to those beginning their spiritual journey or those that might relate to your time of darkness. You can share how you grew your faith. In doing so, you give a voice to your imperfections and will find it liberating. I'm betting people won't condemn you at all. You may earn their respect – this is the freedom I'm describing."

The Pastor paused to assess Harrison's understanding, then continued. "Think about the scars that Jesus received. His back was mutilated, his forehead was pierced with thorns, his hands and feet were punctured with nails that bound Him to the cross."

"What are you saying?"

"I'm saying Jesus has more scars than we can imagine and look at what He did with those scars. He used them to show God's love for His people. We, as Christians, couldn't experience God's promise without the scars of His son."

"I suppose that's true," said Harrison.

"Did you listen to anything I said today during the sermon?" Pastor Bob joked trying to bring a smile to the young man's face.

He continued, "If you think about it, Jesus needed those scars because without them, we have no Gospel. We have no good news to share. It's precisely His scars that show us how much God, The Father, loves us. God sacrificed His only son so you could have eternal life."

Pastor Bob wanted Harrison to understand the parallel to his own struggle with his final thought.

"You have scars Harrison. They're emotional, but they still hurt the same. Jesus used His scars to tell His story to the world. He recognized that His death, as a result of those scars, was necessary to bring greater good beyond Himself."

Harrison knew this was the story of the Gospel. Pastor Bob presented it in a way he never considered before. He sat silently still when the clergy posed a challenge.

"What are you going to do with your scars? Are you going to hide them in shame, or will you give them a voice to show how God used you during your time of great trial? Does the story become your testimony?"

Harrison dropped his head. The burden he felt was being lifted away bringing new understanding and perspective.

He was still reluctant to share his story. This would take some time to digest. He spent the following week praying, and during those moments, even wrestling with God.

How can I give God what He wants without telling others?, he tried to negotiate. *What if I just accept the fact that I've been damaged, and I live a good life as a good husband and father? Can I be a witness to the Gospel some other way?*

Harrison tried again and again through conversations with God. There had to be a negotiable middle-ground, but no matter how hard he tried, he knew it was short of what God intended.

The time would come when he needed to reveal his scars to others if he were going to pay witness to the Gospel. It was the giant that needed to be slain.

He needed to get over his fear and the only way to do that was to embrace the scars as a symbol of how God used them to make him a stronger follower of Jesus Christ.

Forgiving himself and shedding his shame to live a life of freedom seemed like a better option. As he thought about it, he felt empowered.

THIRTY-ONE

"Make level paths for your feet and take only ways that are firm."

THE TIMELINESS OF THE SERMON SERIES DIDN'T GO UNNOTICED BY Harrison. People often posted on social media about God's perfect timing, but he never understood it until now.

For Christians, forgiveness appeared to be a central concept. Understanding God's forgiveness and forgiving oneself proved to be a great start to the life of freedom, which Pastor Bob described. Harrison was not prepared for the impact that the two sermons and discussions with the Pastor would have on him.

He was aware of the upcoming sermon *Forgiving Others*. Harrison knew what this meant – God was challenging him to forgive his father.

Harrison shook his head each time he mentally tried to grasp the concept. After all his father put him and Claire through, Harrison didn't feel as if he was ready to let it go. He wasn't sure his father deserved forgiveness.

Harrison reflected and recalled a conversation he had with his dad during the prison's visitation hours. Harlan told his son that he didn't do anything wrong, and he was only following the rules written by Medicare. His father wasn't sorry, and Harlan continued to say that they made an example out of him.

Don't people who deserve forgiveness need to be sorry? Harrison thought.

Harrison remembered a time before his father's arrest when Harlan valued money before family. He used people as collateral. Harlan leaned on false friendships and possessions, drifting further away from family. Harrison drifted away too, but only because he became tired of trying.

Harrison knew both of them missed out on a father and son bond that could have been much more.

He considered Becca and other children that Harrison and Claire might be blessed with someday. Harlan didn't give up a relationship with only Harrison, Harlan gave up a relationship with his grandchild.

The younger Marks felt as if his father took a baseball bat to his kneecaps.

Who does that to their son? he questioned forcefully.

Harrison was angry, and he wanted his father to pay the price for hurting him.

On that particular Sunday morning, when Pastor Bob spoke about *Forgiving Others*, the pastor made the dynamics of forgiving easy to understand.

"Dr. Timothy Keller," Pastor Bob began, "says when speaking about forgiveness, Jesus often speaks in terms of debt. In other words, when people wrong us, there is a sense they now owe us. Their wrong-doing has created an obligation they must re-pay."

Harrison was fully onboard with this sermon so far. He was glad he came. He gave Claire a nudge with his elbow to get her attention and followed with a nod of approval regarding Pastor Bob's opening comment.

"To forgive then," Pastor Bob continued, "according to Keller, means giving up the right to seek repayment from that person who harmed you. Forgiveness is a voluntary act of sacrifice."

Claire gave a nudge back to Harrison. She smiled and nodded her approval toward Pastor Bob's follow-up statement. Harrison didn't see the humor.

Once again, he delivered a stirring sermon. Unfortunately, Harrison missed a lot of the context because he drifted to focus on his struggles.

Claire was smart enough to drive separately this week. Still seated, she smiled at Harrison, knowing he was going to stay behind. She retrieved Becca from the nursery and headed home.

After the congregation cleared, Pastor Bob motioned Harrison to follow him to his office.

Harrison never bothered with a greeting once they sat down. "What if I'm not ready to forgive?"

Pastor Bob remained silent while staring across his desk. "By choosing not to forgive, you are harming yourself."

"Why?"

Pastor Bob was ready to answer. "Forgiveness is a gift, but if you think it's a gift to your father, you're wrong. Forgiveness is a gift to yourself."

"But, how?"

"By hanging on to your anger, you rob yourself of the joy that God has planned for you. When you hold on to anger, you're saying that your contempt for someone is more important than your happiness. Doesn't that seem silly when you think about it?"

"I can't let him hurt my family or me again," Harrison said.

The Pastor had Harrison right where he wanted him. "Can I ask you a question?"

"Sure."

"Did you think you would go through this life without experiencing pain?"

"I don't know," Harrison responded.

"Jesus endured tremendous pain. As a Christian, what makes you think you wouldn't experience pain in your lifetime?"

It was a new perspective that Harrison had not considered.

Pastor Bob continued. "I have another question. How can you be so selfish?"

"What? How am I selfish?" He realized he snapped and tried to settle himself down. "He did this to me. I have a right to be angry."

"Maybe," Pastor Bob shrugged. "But Jesus died to save us from our sins. You and I hung Him on that cross, Harrison. Jesus didn't die for the sinners of the world 2,000 years ago. He died for the future sinners of the world as well. That means He had to give up His life for you. He paid the ultimate sacrifice."

Pastor Bob's words were powerful. Harrison's legs and arms froze and became extremely heavy to move. He felt tied to the chair with no ability to move, and deep remorse set in.

"God was willing to give His only Son in sacrifice to show his love for you. Jesus was willing to accept His fate for your sins showing true forgiveness. He paid your debt, Harrison."

"So, I'll ask again. Are you selfish when you withhold forgiveness when so much forgiveness is given to you?"

Harrison dropped his head. It felt as if the room was silent for an eternity.

Pastor Bob waited. He could see the truth penetrating Harrison's heart and mind. Harrison's face was filled with sorrow, and he looked like a child who learned a hard lesson from a parent.

He added, "Forgiving others doesn't always mean you need to rebuild the relationship. It simply allows you to stop being angry and live the life God intended. Are you ready to live the good life?"

Harrison finally responded only to say, "Thank you."

He stood from the chair to shake his hand. The young man exited the office and closed the door behind him.

Harrison shuffled out of the church, across the parking lot, and into his car. He sat in silence.

He was uncertain how to feel. Pastor Bob's words hit him hard. Should he accept the truth and choose to forgive, or should he now hold a grudge toward both his father and the clergy? The second choice seemed like a good option at the moment.

Over the next few weeks, Claire watched her husband. She knew his classic response was to retreat when he had things to sort out. She didn't anticipate that he would walk through the door and start talking the way she might have done. She was correct when she assumed this would take some time.

EPILOGUE

"Do not forget my teachings, but keep my commands in your heart, for they will prolong your life many years and bring you prosperity."

HARRISON'S FATHER WAS RELEASED FROM PRISON AFTER SERVING three years on a five-year sentence. He returned to Indianapolis to live with his now 94-year-old mother in her two-bedroom apartment.

Victoria filed for divorce shortly after Harlan was sent to the Morgantown, West Virginia prison. Not surprisingly, the family never heard from her again.

But for Harrison, a final hurdle remained. He felt the need to reconcile with his father.

Harrison didn't experience a revelation or have a bombshell conversation with a friend telling him this was necessary. It was out of respect for his grandmother.

The reconciliation was a process, and both Harlan and Harrison pursued. Although they didn't agree on the case's details, they agreed to move forward in a relationship.

During the following days and years, Harrison realized what was important in his life. While it made each day more rewarding, it didn't always make it easier. He still faced challenges. The transition from believing in God and following God was a process. Some days were harder than others; some days seemed impossible.

It was different now. Harrison made a conscious decision to forgive. It meant making a choice every day to put down the burden he had been carrying for so long.

Harrison understood forgiveness and allowed himself to stop holding anger, resentment, shame, and pain that interrupted what God intended for his life. It gave him the freedom to enjoy his time with Claire and Becca, and now his little boy.

Harrison and Claire developed deeper friendships with people at church. They found other couples who set an example of a Godly marriage. Harrison and Claire knew what they wanted their marriage to resemble. Dinners and campfires were surrounded by friends on a spiritual level. He and Claire felt loved.

During the early years in Madison, Harrison kept the story to himself. It was too difficult to discuss. It wasn't until dinner with a couple many years later that he felt an unsuspected tug at his heart.

Harrison always took pride walking away from a conversation learning more about the other individual than they learned about him. He asked questions as he was curious to learn about his friend's background, family, and most importantly, what motivated the person.

This night was different. The Marks friends asked Harrison about moving to Madison, Indiana – what brought the couple to this small town? For years he told people it was his job. But this night, their friends wanted to dig deeper.

Harrison looked at Claire, and she smiled, waiting for her husband to respond. He felt an overwhelming sense of peace and safety. He realized it was time to share the truth.

"You want to know why we're here?" Harrison asked. Without telling them anything, a burden was lifted. It must have been God's way of telling him "It's time".

"Let me run to the restroom before I start because this could take a while."

Harrison excused himself from the table.

He heard Claire whisper as he walked away, "He's been needing to talk about this for a long time."

Harrison walked into the restroom and closed the door. He stood in front of the mirror, gazed at his reflection, and recognized a new man. It was a different person in the reflection – different than the man he saw in the courtroom bathroom many years ago. Harrison had allowed God to break into his time and space to mold him as a man of faith, a husband, and a father.

The pain he experienced lead him on the path to a greater authority where he began to move toward a discipleship while stripping away the things of the world.

The young man, now stepping into the role God intended, no longer felt animosity toward his father. He no longer held his father responsible to the emotions he was feeling. He found compassion for a man that was in search of the same forgiveness and peace offered to him through God.

Harrison began to understand spiritual discipline. A discipline that offered freedom from unbearable chains. A joyful obedience to God, while always a work in progress, provided the pursuit of happiness that every man chases, but can't often find.

He was in love with a God that relentlessly pursued him and loved him unconditionally, rather than a god that required him to reach helplessly for approval. For God already made the sacrifice of his only son. What additional proof did Harrison need God to reveal to show how much He wanted him and called him His own?

It was a beginning for Harrison, not an end. His journey opened a new pathway that began to reveal his God-given gifts so he could give back to God through purposeful discipleship breathing spiritual life into others.

This time he knew he had the One that was *for* him, not *against* him. It was time to show his faith in God. It wasn't Harrison's strength that would enable him to share the story – it was God's strength within him. While his father's reign had fallen, it was now God's reign falling upon him like redeeming grace.

God was the hero. The testimony belonged to Harrison. The story belonged to God.